AI Revolution & Future of Health

Pradip Kumar Ray

&

Pragyan Ray

Dedication

To the unwavering spirit of innovation and human curiosity, we dedicate this book to the countless pioneers and visionaries who have paved the way for technological marvels and advancements in healthcare.

To our families, for their endless support and encouragement, particularly Babli Roy, whose thoughtful insights continue to inspire.

To the youth of today and the leaders of tomorrow, may you harness the power of Artificial Intelligence to build a healthier, more equitable future for all.

— Pradip Kumar Ray & Pragyan Ray

Acknowledgement

The journey of creating this book, *AI Revolution & Future of Health*, has been one of learning, collaboration, and discovery. We are deeply grateful to everyone who has contributed to its realization.

First and foremost, we express our heartfelt gratitude to Smt. Babli Roy, whose meticulous manuscript reading and insightful suggestions were invaluable during this process. Her unwavering support and encouragement have been a guiding light.

We extend our sincere thanks to Sonali Roy, the editor of this work, for her keen eye, creative input, and dedication to perfecting the content. Her editorial expertise has been instrumental in bringing clarity and precision to the narrative.

A special mention goes to the innumerable researchers, innovators, and medical professionals who are tirelessly advancing the boundaries of artificial intelligence and healthcare. Your work has been a source of inspiration for us.

Finally, we acknowledge the unconditional love and support of our families and friends, who have been our pillars of strength throughout this endeavor. Your faith in us keeps our aspirations alive.

We hope this book inspires its readers to embrace the potential of artificial intelligence in transforming healthcare and envisioning a better future for humanity.

— *Pradip Kumar Ray & Pragyan Ray*

First Impression by the Manuscript Reader

It has been an enlightening experience to review the manuscript of *AI Revolution & Future of Health*. This book delves into a profound and timely subject, exploring the transformative potential of artificial intelligence in reshaping healthcare systems across the globe.

The authors, Pradip Kumar Ray and Pragyan Ray, have successfully blended their expertise and visionary thinking to present a comprehensive and accessible narrative. The content is not only informative but also thought-provoking, offering readers a nuanced perspective on how AI can revolutionize diagnostics, treatment, and healthcare management.

What sets this book apart is its seamless integration of technological insights with practical applications in health sciences. It highlights real-world examples, forward-thinking innovations, and ethical considerations, making it both relevant and relatable for a wide range of audiences.

The editorial contributions of Sonali Roy shine through in the manuscript's clarity, coherence, and refined structure. Her meticulous attention to detail has elevated the book to an exceptional standard.

As a manuscript reader, I am deeply impressed by the depth of research, the originality of ideas, and the vision that this work encapsulates. *AI Revolution & Future of Health* is a significant contribution to contemporary literature, offering valuable guidance and inspiration to professionals, researchers, and anyone curious about the future of health in the age of AI.

— Smt. Babli Roy
Manuscript Reader

Preface

The world stands at the cusp of a technological transformation that promises to redefine the way we live, work, and care for our health. Artificial Intelligence (AI) has emerged as a driving force behind innovations across industries, and its potential to revolutionize healthcare is unparalleled. With this vision in mind, we present *AI Revolution & Future of Health*. This book is the culmination of our combined passion for science, technology, and its profound impact on human well-being. Over the past few years, we have witnessed remarkable progress in AI, from advanced diagnostic tools and personalized treatments to groundbreaking research in genomics and robotics. Yet, these advancements also raise important questions about ethics, accessibility, and the readiness of our societies to embrace this change.

In crafting this work, we sought to address these challenges while celebrating the limitless possibilities AI offers to the healthcare domain. This book is designed to serve as both a comprehensive guide and a source of inspiration for professionals, students, researchers, and lay readers who are curious about the convergence of AI and healthcare. We owe a deep debt of gratitude to Smt. Babli Roy, whose thoughtful manuscript reading and valuable feedback have enriched this book. Her insights brought clarity and depth to our ideas. We also extend our heartfelt thanks to our editor, Sonali Roy, for her diligent efforts in shaping the structure and ensuring the narrative is as engaging as it is informative.

This book would not have been possible without the support and encouragement of our families, who have stood by us through this journey. It is our sincere hope that *AI Revolution & Future of Health* will inspire you to think boldly, innovate courageously, and contribute to building a healthier, more equitable future for humanity.

— **Pradip Kumar Ray & Pragyan Ray**
December 2024

Permission & Copyright

No part of this book may be copied, translated, or reproduced in any form without the express written permission of the author. Unauthorized reproduction or use of any part of this book will result in legal action. Although every precaution has been taken in the preparation of this book, the publisher assumes no responsibility for errors, omissions, or damages that may arise from the use of the information contained herein. If you encounter any doubts or uncertainties regarding the content of this book, we strongly advise consulting with subject matter experts to prevent any potential misunderstandings or losses.

This book has been published following diligent efforts to ensure its accuracy and quality, with the author's approval. However, the author and publisher disclaim any liability for any loss, damage, or disruption caused by errors or omissions, whether arising from negligence, accident, or any other cause. While every effort has been made to avoid mistakes or omissions, the book is sold with the understanding that neither the author, publisher, nor printer shall be held liable for any errors nor omissions in the content, nor for actions taken or advice followed based on the material. In the event of any defect in printing or binding, the publisher's liability is limited to replacing the defective copy with another available copy.

Pradip Kumar Ray & Pragyan Ray
First Edition: December29, 2024
Copyright © 2024 Pradip Kumar Ray
All Rights Reserved   -Publisher & Author

Author Introduction

Pradip Kumar Ray

The author retired from his long-standing career in banking, with his final post being Chief Manager (Offing) at the Purshura Branch of State Bank of India (SBI). Throughout his career, he served in various roles such as Branch Manager, HR Manager, System Manager etc , gaining a wealth of experience across multiple banking functions. During this time, he also nurtured a hobby of discovering magic and writing, which led to the publication of his first book, "*Prerana*" in 2013. His written works have been featured in several prominent newspapers and magazines, and his expertise in magic earned him a mention in the *Magicians' World Directory*.

In terms of academic qualifications, the author holds a BSc (Honours in Physics), MSc (Computer Science), and a Post Graduate Diploma in Computer Applications (PGDCA). He is a Cisco Certified Network Associate (CCNA)(Global) and a Certified Associate of the Indian Institute of Banking (CAIIB). Additionally, he has completed various certification courses in photo, video, and audio editing, animation, hardware, cobol programming, "Praggya" Hindi courses, and a certification course from the Insurance Regulatory and Development Authority of India (IRDAI).

Post-retirement, the author has remained active by collaborating with different academies as a subject-matter expert in banking. He also runs a YouTube channel, Facebook page, website, and blog, where he continues to engage his audience. Additionally, the author contributes to stock photography, writes articles, and publishes his own books. To date, he has authored over 120 books, many of which are available through national and international online platforms. Some of his published works include:

In Bengali: 1) Prerana 2) Anuprerana 3) Chetana 4) Mahabharate Ki Ki Tathya Chitrita Achhe JA Ajo Prasangik? 5) Puran Kahineer Antarnihita Artha 5) Ramayaner Ajana Tathya 6) Ki Vabe Manabik Gunabalir Jagaran Sambhab Ja Antarer Alo Jwalay 7) Manab Monobiganer Upar Bhagbat Grrtar Gavir Pravab 8) Karna O Ekalabya – Mahabharater Na Bala Galpa 9) Dhurta Shakuni-Mahabharater Na Bala Galpa 10) Manabatar Pujari Swalpa Prichita Bharatiyer Kahinee 11) Ashepasher Gachh Gachhalir Soundarya O Oshadhi Gun. 12) Jana Manusher Ajana Kahinee 13) Baba Mane- Maa Mane–14) Kalpanay, Kheyalr O Kathane Corona 15) Nijer Madhyei Nije 16) Bharater Sampurna Binamulyer Besarkari Hospital 17) Krishna – Mahabharater Paradoxical O Jatil Charitra 18) ShibaPuran :Adhyatya O Bigyaner Apurba Sammilan.

In English: 1) How to Write Banking Letters (For Bankers & Customers) More than 120 Relevant sample letters. 2) How to Write an Email (Ethics, Examples & Samples of Emails).3) GENERAL APTITUDE (CSIR Net-Previous Q & A with explanation and hint to solve) 4) Certificate Examination of Business Correspondent 5) MCQ with Answers for BC & BF Examination 6) Certificate Examination for Debt Recovery Agent of IIBF 7) Secrets of Motivation & Inspiration 8) How to Improve Your Mental Strength 9) Totally Free Best Private Hospitals in India 10) The Story of a Little-Known Indian Worshiper of Humanity 11) Unpopular but Attracting with Historical Interest Tourist Place in

Bardhhaman. 12) 'Corona' in Imagination, Troll & Mimes. 13) Short Stories and Tales 14) How Human Qualities Awakening Possible which Ignites Light in the Heart 15) Karna & Ekalavya – The Untold Story of the Mahabharata 16) Transform Your Thinking, Transform Your Life 17) Unknown Facts Of Epic Ramayana 18) Ekalavya – The Untold Story of the Mahabharata19) Overcoming Adversity: A Journey of Love and Resilience 20) Meg's Mission: Pushing the Boundaries of Healthcare 21) Ideas to develop a multi-user Portable medical devise related to blood for use at home by beginners and Researchers 22) How to Prepare Delicious Recipes for Every Occasion, The Bengali Bites 23) The Inner Light Reflections(Compassion, Resilience, Empathy) 24) Perseverance: The Key to Unlocking Your Potential 25) More than a Hundred Inventing Ideas on Microfluidics 26) Awakening Your Inner Drive: The Power of Motivation, Inspiration, and Consciousness 27) The Lost Planet 28) Unleashing the Power of Supreme Energy 29)Folding Space: The Quest for Three-Dimensional Folding 30)From Despair to Triumph: A Tale of Courage and Hope 31) The Unseen Hero (A Journey of Self-Discovery) 32) AI Magic: Free Tools for Perfecting Your Images (A Step-By-Step Guide) 33)The Untold Story of Karna: A Tale of Perseverance and Determination 33) Dad Means–Mom Means—34) Fundamentals of IT 35) How to do Your Life as much as Simple 36) Step By Step Guide (INB,CDM & ATM of Axis Bank) 37) Step By Step Guide (INB,CDM & ATM of SBI) 38) Durgapujor Prakkale 39) Step by Step Guide: SBI Credit Card 40) Step By Step Guide: SBI Internet Banking 41) Keys to Success: Lessons for Reaching Goals and Overcoming Challenges 42)Krishna: The Paradoxical and Complex Character in the Mahabharata 43) Comparative Analysis of Six World-Famous Ancient Epics 44) Journey to Ancient Greece: Discovering the

Iliad and Odyssey 45) Echoes of the North: Kalevala Rediscovered 46) Digital Banking Ready Reference for Customer 47) A Comprehensive Guide on IBPS Preli Clerk Exam, 48) NEET Exam: Biology Mastering Concepts with 1200+ MCQs & Answers 49) Indian Economy and Indian Financial System (IE & IFS) 50)Competitive Examination of Railways: Unlocking Your Path to a Rewarding Career,51)Comparative Analysis of Six World-Famous Ancient Epics 52) Beyond the Horizon: Unveiling Motivation, Awakening Light, and the Journey of Conscious Empathy 53) Principles & Practices of Banking (PPB) 54) Accounting and Financial Management for Bankers (AFM) 55) Retail Banking and Wealth Management (RBM) 56) JAIIB ALL IN ONE 57) Timeless Teaching of the Bhagbad Gita on Human Psychology 58) Exploring the Theatrical and Cinematic Worlds of Ramayana 59) The Divine Threads (Krishna's Influence in the Mahabharata) 60) The Mahabharata and Its Significance in Contemporary Society 61) Basics of Information Technology 62) Legends of Ramayana: A Timeless Epic 63) BC & BF Exam Prep: Multiple Choice Questions with Answers 64) Aspire, Achieve, Inspire - A Journey to Fulfilling Dreams 65) Scrolls of Health : Exploring Ancient Medical Manuscripts 66) Exploring Vedic Thought From Knowledge to Liberation 67) Evolution of Bengali Literary Heritage 68) International Literary Heritage 69) Dad Means Dad: The Unexplored Hero 70) Mom Means Mom : the Unconditional Eternal Love 71) Self Within Myself 72) Exploring the Comparative Analysis of Six Legendary Epics 73) Durga Puja Narrative: A Celebration in Bengal 74) Bengali Dishes Classic Modern Twists 75) Rise and Shine : Daily Habits for Student Success 76) Ignite Your Spark 77) From Loser to Legend: The Power of Motivation 78) Exploring the Theatrical and Cinematic Worlds of Ramayana 79) The Inherent Meaning of Mythology 80) The

Mahabharata and Its Significance in Contemporary Society 81) Krishna : The Divine Threads of the Mahabharata 82) How to Develop Your Mental Strength (Motivational & Inspirational) 83) The Mindful Parent Nurturing Emotional Intelligence in Children 84) Inspirational Insights For a Fulfilled Life 85) Aspire, Achieve, Inspire - A Journey to Fulfilling Dreams 86) The Divine Threads (Krishna's Influence in the Mahabharata) etc.

In Hindi: 1) Prerak Koushal Me Sudhar Kaise Kare. 2) Chhatra Aour Bankaro Ke Lie Banking. 3) "Corona" – Kathan, Troll & Mimes. 4) Oitihasik Akarshak Parjatan Sthal, Burdwan 5) Apni Manasik Shakti Ka Bikash Kaise Kre 6) Sambandha Bipanan Shikhne Ka Sabse Achchha Tarika 7) Share Trading Me Monobigyan Aur Anushashan Kaise Shikhe 8) Unnata Video Marketing Kaise Kare 9) SEO Keya Hai Aur Kaise Kam Karta Hai 10) Banking Patra Kaise Likhe? 11) Karna O Ekalabya – Mahabharat Ki Unkahi Kahinee 12) Naye Sight Se ISBN Kaise Prapta Kare? 13) Alpa Gyat Bharatiya Upasak Ki Kahani (Series-1,2&3) 14) Krishna- Mahabharat Me BirodhBhashi O Jatil Charitra 15) Chhay Bishwa Prasiddha Prachin Mahakabya Ka Tulanatmak Bishleshan etc. Publisher (Pkrbur Publication).

Website: https://pkrbur.com & https://bit.ly/PKRBOOK
Email: pkrbur@gmail.com & pradip.ray1911@gmail.com

Author Introduction

Pragyan Ray

Author is an engineer by training, currently engaged in multidisciplinary research. Author mainly focuses in the field of biotechnology, medical device innovation and biomedical engineering. He has honed his skills in Pharmaceutical Biotechnology during graduation and post-graduation degree; and currently working as a PhD scholar at NIT Rourkela in the area of microfluidics & biomedical engineering. Apart from research, the author has experience of working in the formulation R&D in the corporate sector.

The author has completed certificate course on "Drug Development" from the University of California San Diego and also completed another online certificate course on "Design and Interpretation of Clinical Trials" from Johns Hopkins University. The author has presented poster in numerous conferences and successfully participated in different workshops.

He is also actively engaged in conference arrangement, research and start-up proposal evaluation. Being able to reach to millions of people through innovation is the sole motivator of the author. The author believes, addressing the challenges at grass root level, is the key to achieve success in any area of society, be it in terms of education or health.

Several articles have already been published in various National and International Research Magazines and also his first Print Book "NEET Exam: Biology Mastering Concepts with 1200+ MCQs & Answers" have published on 2nd August'2023 which is now available at Different Online Stores. In addition to that he have also authored for the Books Cordyceps Insight (Nature's Hidden Miracle & Step by Step Guide to Growing It at Home) and Saffron Smart Aeroponic Cultivation at Home(Detail Description and Step by Step Guide).

Email: pragyan.ray1998@gmail.com
Link at LinkedIn: https://bit.ly/1998PR

-Publisher

Pkrbur Publication

PKRBUR PUBLICATION
A Platform for Emerging Writers ®

A Platform for Emerging Writers

In the vast landscape of publishing, there lies a hidden treasure trove of untapped talent, waiting to be discovered. PKRBUR Publication emerges as a beacon for those new and energetic voices, whose literary endeavours have yet to find their way into the limelight. With a mission to unearth the raw creativity and unique perspectives of emerging writers, PKRBUR Publication stands as a champion of innovation and diversity in the literary world. Founded on the belief that every writer deserves a chance to share their story, PKRBUR Publication offers a platform specifically tailored to the needs of burgeoning authors. Whether hindered by lack of exposure, limited resources, or simply the daunting nature of the publishing industry, many talented writers find themselves overlooked or discouraged from pursuing their dreams. PKRBUR Publication aims to break down these barriers, providing a supportive environment where creativity can flourish.

At the heart of PKRBUR Publication's ethos is a commitment to showcasing a diverse range of voices and perspectives. In a world where mainstream publishing often favours established authors or certain genres, PKRBUR Publication embraces the richness of human experience in all its forms. From thought-provoking essays to captivating fiction, from scholarly research to experimental poetry, every voice has the potential to resonate with readers and spark meaningful conversations. One of the hallmarks of PKRBUR Publication is its dedication to nurturing talent from the ground up. Recognizing that many emerging writers may not have access to traditional avenues of publication, PKRBUR Publication offers comprehensive support throughout the publishing process. From manuscript development and editing to cover design and marketing, writers receive personalized guidance every step of the way. This hands-on approach not only ensures the highest quality publications but also empowers writers to take ownership of their creative journey.

Furthermore, PKRBUR Publication operates with a commitment to transparency and fairness. Authors retain control over their work and receive equitable compensation for their contributions. By fostering a culture of respect and collaboration, PKRBUR Publication seeks to build lasting relationships with its authors and readers alike. In an ever-changing literary landscape, PKRBUR Publication stands as a beacon of hope for aspiring writers everywhere. With its unwavering dedication to fostering talent and amplifying diverse voices, PKRBUR Publication is poised to make a lasting impact on the world of publishing. As the literary community continues to evolve, PKRBUR Publication remains steadfast in its mission to champion the next generation of writers and thinkers.

Website: https://pkrbur.com & https://bit.ly/PKRBOOK
Email: pkrbur@gmail.com & pradip.ray1911@gmail.com

Part-A (AI in Healthcare)
Chapter 1: Introduction to AI in Healthcare

Understanding AI and Its Applications in Healthcare

Artificial Intelligence (AI) has become an essential component in the evolution of healthcare, revolutionizing the way medical professionals diagnose and treat patients. Its applications range from enhancing diagnostic accuracy to streamlining treatment planning. With the ability to process vast amounts of data quickly and efficiently, AI systems can identify patterns and correlations that human practitioners might overlook. This capability is particularly valuable in fields such as radiology and pathology, where AI algorithms analyze medical images and laboratory results to assist healthcare providers in making informed decisions.

In diagnostics, AI tools are increasingly utilized for medical imaging analysis. Algorithms trained on thousands of images can detect anomalies, such as tumors or fractures, often with a higher degree of precision than traditional methods. This not only expedites the diagnostic process but also reduces the likelihood of human error. Additionally, AI systems are employed in predictive analytics, allowing for early identification of potential disease outbreaks by analyzing trends and patterns in health data. Such proactive measures can significantly enhance public health responses and resource allocation.

Treatment planning has also seen tremendous advancements through AI applications. Machine learning models can analyze a patient's medical history, genetic information, and current health status to recommend personalized treatment options tailored to the individual's needs. This approach not only improves the effectiveness of therapies but also minimizes adverse effects, as treatments can be better aligned with a patient's unique biological makeup. Furthermore, AI-driven personalized medicine is becoming increasingly prevalent, where treatments are customized based on genetic profiles, leading to more effective interventions. Patient monitoring has been transformed by AI technologies, which enable continuous tracking of health metrics through wearable devices and mobile applications. These tools use real-time health data analytics to provide insights into a patient's condition, allowing for timely interventions when abnormalities are detected. Virtual health assistants powered by AI are also enhancing patient engagement, offering reminders for medication, providing information about symptoms, and facilitating communication with healthcare providers. This ongoing support can lead to improved adherence to treatment plans and better overall health outcomes.

Finally, the integration of AI into drug discovery and development is streamlining the process of bringing new medications to market. By utilizing AI algorithms to analyze existing drug data and predict potential drug interactions, researchers can significantly reduce the time and cost associated with traditional drug development. Additionally, automated workflow solutions in hospitals enhance operational efficiency, allowing healthcare professionals to focus more on patient care rather than administrative tasks. Overall, as AI continues to evolve, its applications in healthcare promise to enhance diagnostics, treatment, and patient support, ultimately leading to a healthier future for all.

The Evolution of Healthcare Technologies

The evolution of healthcare technologies has dramatically transformed the way health is managed and delivered, particularly with the advent of artificial intelligence (AI). In recent decades, advancements in computing power and data analytics have enabled healthcare professionals to harness vast amounts of data for better patient outcomes. From the early days of electronic health records to today's sophisticated AI-driven diagnostic tools, the trajectory of healthcare technology reveals a commitment to improving accuracy, efficiency, and accessibility in health management.

AI in diagnostics has emerged as a game-changer, allowing for quicker and more accurate identification of health conditions. Traditional diagnostic methods often relied on manual interpretation of data, which could lead to human error and delayed treatment. With machine learning algorithms analyzing medical images and lab results, healthcare providers can now detect diseases like cancer or neurological disorders with remarkable precision. These tools not only enhance diagnostic accuracy but also reduce the time needed for results, facilitating timely interventions that can save lives.The impact of AI extends beyond diagnostics into treatment planning and personalized medicine. With the capability to analyze vast datasets, AI can identify patterns and correlations that may not be apparent to human clinicians. This enables the development of tailored treatment plans that consider individual patient profiles, genetic makeup, and lifestyle factors. AI-driven platforms are now being utilized to recommend the most effective therapies and interventions, thus optimizing outcomes while minimizing side effects. As a result, patients receive more targeted care, enhancing overall treatment efficacy.

Patient monitoring has also been revolutionized by AI technologies, which provide continuous, real-time data about an individual's health status. Wearable devices and mobile health applications collect data on vital signs, activity levels, and other health metrics, allowing for proactive management of chronic conditions. AI algorithms can analyze this data to predict potential health declines, alerting healthcare providers and patients to take preventive measures. This shift towards proactive health management not only improves individual patient care but also reduces hospital admissions and healthcare costs.

As we look to the future, the integration of AI in healthcare will continue to evolve, offering new opportunities for treatment and support. AI-powered virtual health assistants are already enhancing patient engagement, providing instant access to health information and support. Chatbots for mental health are making therapy more accessible, offering users immediate assistance and resources. Predictive analytics for disease outbreaks can help public health officials respond more effectively to emerging health threats. The ongoing development of AI technologies promises to further enhance rehabilitation programs and streamline hospital workflows, ultimately leading to a more efficient and patient-centered healthcare system.

The Importance of AI in Modern Medicine

The integration of artificial intelligence in modern medicine is revolutionizing the healthcare landscape, providing unprecedented opportunities for improving patient outcomes and enhancing the efficiency of medical practices. AI technologies are increasingly being utilized in various aspects of healthcare, from diagnostics to treatment planning and patient monitoring. This evolution is not merely a trend; it represents a fundamental shift in how healthcare is delivered, making it more proactive, precise, and personalized. As AI continues to develop, its significance in medicine becomes more apparent, promising a future where healthcare is more responsive to individual needs and public health challenges.

One of the most significant areas where AI is making an impact is in diagnostics. AI algorithms can analyze vast amounts of medical data, including imaging studies, lab results, and patient histories, to identify patterns that may be overlooked by human practitioners. This capability enhances diagnostic accuracy, leading to earlier detection of diseases such as cancer, where timely intervention is crucial. AI-powered medical imaging analysis, for instance, can assist radiologists by highlighting anomalies in scans, improving the speed of diagnosis and allowing for more effective treatment plans tailored to the specific conditions of patients.

In treatment planning, AI's ability to process and analyze data enables healthcare providers to develop personalized treatment strategies. Through machine learning algorithms, AI can examine the effectiveness of different treatments across diverse patient populations, leading to more informed decisions based on individual health profiles. This personalized medicine approach ensures that patients receive therapies that are most likely to be effective, reducing the trial-and-error nature of treatment. Furthermore, AI-driven predictive analytics can forecast potential disease outbreaks, allowing health systems to prepare and allocate resources more efficiently, ultimately improving community health outcomes.

Patient monitoring is another critical domain where AI is proving invaluable. With the advent of wearable technology and real-time health data analytics, patients can be continuously monitored for various health metrics. AI systems can identify trends and anomalies in this data, alerting healthcare providers to potential issues before they escalate. Additionally, virtual health assistants and chatbots are enhancing patient engagement, providing timely support and information, and helping individuals manage their health proactively. These tools not only empower patients but also alleviate some of the burdens on healthcare professionals, enabling them to focus on more complex cases. As AI continues to advance, its applications in drug discovery and development, genetic disorder identification, and rehabilitation programs are set to transform healthcare further. The capabilities of AI to analyze genetic data can lead to breakthroughs in understanding hereditary conditions, while automated workflow solutions streamline hospital operations, improving the overall patient experience. The integration of AI in mental health support through chatbots offers a new avenue for providing assistance, making mental health resources more accessible. Collectively, these innovations underscore the importance of AI in modern medicine, paving the way for a healthier future where technology and human expertise work hand in hand to enhance care.

Chapter 2: AI in Diagnostics

The Role of AI in Early Disease Detection

The integration of artificial intelligence (AI) in early disease detection represents a transformative leap in healthcare, providing both patients and providers with tools that can identify health issues before they progress. Early detection is critical for conditions such as cancer, diabetes, and cardiovascular diseases, where timely intervention can significantly improve outcomes. AI systems utilize vast amounts of data from medical records, genetic information, and even lifestyle factors to identify patterns that may elude human observation. By leveraging machine learning algorithms, these systems can analyze complex datasets to predict the likelihood of disease, enabling proactive management of health issues.

AI-powered medical imaging analysis is one of the most promising applications in early disease detection. Advanced algorithms can process and analyze imaging data more accurately and quickly than traditional methods. For instance, AI tools have shown remarkable success in detecting tumors in radiology scans, helping radiologists make faster and more accurate diagnoses. This not only enhances the precision of diagnostic imaging but also facilitates timely treatment decisions, ultimately improving patient outcomes and reducing healthcare costs associated with advanced disease stages.

Predictive analytics plays a vital role in anticipating disease outbreaks and identifying at-risk populations. By analyzing historical health data, environmental factors, and social determinants of health, AI can model potential future outbreaks of infectious diseases. This capability is particularly important in the context of global health, where early warning systems can help allocate resources effectively and implement preventive measures. By identifying trends and patterns, AI empowers public health officials and healthcare providers to respond swiftly, mitigating the impact of diseases before they spread widely.

Personalized medicine is another area where AI significantly enhances early disease detection and treatment planning. By analyzing genetic information alongside lifestyle and health data, AI can help identify individuals at higher risk for certain conditions. This individualized approach allows healthcare providers to tailor prevention strategies and treatment plans that are more effective for each patient. For example, AI can predict how a patient may respond to specific treatments based on their genetic makeup, ensuring that interventions are both timely and appropriate.

Finally, the role of AI in patient engagement cannot be overlooked. Virtual health assistants and chatbots provide patients with easy access to information and support, encouraging proactive health management. These tools can remind patients about screenings and check-ups, provide educational resources, and facilitate communication with healthcare providers. By fostering a more engaged patient population, AI helps cultivate a culture of prevention and early detection, ensuring that individuals are not only aware of their health status but also empowered to take action when necessary. The future of health is indeed intertwined with the capabilities of AI, offering unprecedented opportunities for enhancing early disease detection and overall patient care.

AI-Powered Medical Imaging Analysis

AI-powered medical imaging analysis is transforming the landscape of diagnostic medicine by enhancing the accuracy and efficiency of image interpretation. Traditional methods of analyzing medical images, such as X-rays, MRIs, and CT scans, often rely heavily on the expertise of radiologists, which can lead to variability in diagnoses. AI algorithms, trained on vast datasets of medical images, can assist in identifying patterns and anomalies that may be missed by the human eye. This technology not only improves diagnostic accuracy but also significantly reduces the time required for image analysis, allowing healthcare professionals to focus more on patient care. One of the most significant advantages of AI in medical imaging is its ability to learn and adapt over time. Machine learning models can be continuously updated with new data, enhancing their predictive capabilities and ensuring that they remain at the cutting edge of medical knowledge. This adaptability allows for the identification of emerging diseases and conditions, as well as the ability to refine diagnostic processes based on the latest research. As a result, patients benefit from earlier detection of diseases such as cancer, which can lead to better treatment outcomes.

AI-powered imaging analysis also plays a crucial role in the standardization of diagnostic procedures. By providing a consistent, data-driven approach to image interpretation, AI reduces the variability that can occur between different radiologists. This standardization is particularly important in large healthcare systems where multiple practitioners may be involved in patient care. By ensuring that medical images are analyzed using the same criteria and algorithms, AI can help to create a more uniform standard of care across different facilities and providers.

In addition to improving diagnostic accuracy, AI in medical imaging can also facilitate better treatment planning. By analyzing imaging data alongside other patient information, such as genetic profiles and clinical histories, AI can help clinicians develop personalized treatment plans that are tailored to the specific needs of each patient. This holistic approach not only enhances the effectiveness of treatment but also improves patient engagement and satisfaction, as individuals feel more involved in their own healthcare decisions.

As AI continues to evolve, its integration into medical imaging is expected to expand further, opening new frontiers in healthcare. Future developments may include real-time imaging analysis during surgical procedures, enhanced predictive analytics for patient outcomes based on imaging data, and improved training tools for healthcare professionals. By harnessing the power of AI, the medical community can not only improve diagnostics and treatment planning but also ultimately enhance the overall quality of care provided to patients.

Enhancing Lab Test Accuracy with AI

Enhancing lab test accuracy with artificial intelligence represents a significant advancement in the healthcare landscape. As the demand for precise diagnostics continues to rise, AI technologies are proving invaluable in minimizing human error, streamlining processes, and analyzing vast amounts of data. By integrating machine learning algorithms into laboratory practices, healthcare providers can improve the reliability of test results, which is crucial for effective patient care.

This enhancement not only fosters trust in the diagnostic process but also enables clinicians to make more informed decisions based on accurate data.

One of the key benefits of AI in laboratory settings is its ability to analyze complex data sets quickly and efficiently. Traditional lab tests often involve intricate procedures that can lead to variability in results due to human factors. AI systems can standardize these processes, ensuring consistent outcomes by reducing the impact of human error. For instance, machine learning algorithms can be trained on historical lab results to identify patterns and anomalies, allowing for early detection of potential issues and improving the overall quality of diagnostics.

AI also enhances the accuracy of lab tests through predictive analytics. By leveraging historical data and identifying trends, AI can forecast potential health issues before they manifest. This proactive approach enables healthcare providers to intervene earlier, which can be particularly beneficial in identifying conditions that require immediate attention. For example, AI-driven algorithms can analyze genetic data to predict the likelihood of certain diseases, allowing for more personalized testing and treatment plans that cater to individual patient needs.

Moreover, AI can assist in automating routine laboratory workflows, thereby increasing efficiency and accuracy. Automated systems powered by AI can handle sample processing, result validation, and data entry with minimal human intervention. This not only speeds up the testing process but also reduces the chances of clerical errors that often accompany manual handling. With AI managing these repetitive tasks, laboratory professionals can devote more time to complex analyses and patient interaction, ultimately enhancing the quality of care provided.

As we look toward the future of health, the integration of AI into laboratory diagnostics promises to revolutionize how we approach testing and treatment. By enhancing test accuracy, reducing human error, and enabling predictive analytics, AI stands to improve patient outcomes significantly. As individuals take charge of their health, understanding the role of AI in lab testing will empower them to engage more effectively with healthcare providers, ensuring that they receive the most accurate and timely diagnoses possible. This shifts the paradigm from reactive healthcare to a more proactive, personalized approach, paving the way for a healthier future.

Chapter 3: AI in Treatment Planning

Personalized Treatment Plans through AI

Personalized treatment plans through AI represent a transformative shift in how healthcare is delivered, tailoring medical care to the individual rather than relying on a one-size-fits-all approach. By leveraging vast amounts of data from various sources, including genetic information, lifestyle choices, and historical health records, artificial intelligence systems can analyze patterns and predict the most effective treatment strategies for each patient. This individualized approach not only enhances the quality of care but also improves patient outcomes by ensuring that the treatments administered are specifically suited to the unique characteristics of each individual.

The integration of AI in treatment planning begins with data collection and analysis. Machine learning algorithms sift through extensive patient data, identifying trends that may not be apparent to healthcare providers. For instance, AI can analyze genetic data to determine the likelihood of certain diseases, allowing doctors to recommend preventive measures or targeted therapies before symptoms even arise. Additionally, AI-powered medical imaging analysis can provide insights into conditions that may require urgent attention, ensuring that personalized treatment plans are not only effective but timely.

Moreover, AI-driven personalized medicine can adapt to the changing needs of a patient over time. As treatment progresses, ongoing monitoring through real-time health data analytics allows healthcare providers to assess the effectiveness of a given treatment plan and make adjustments as necessary. This dynamic interaction between AI systems and healthcare professionals facilitates a proactive approach to patient care, where adjustments can be made based on the latest data, ensuring that the patient receives the most appropriate therapies at every stage of their healthcare journey.

AI also plays a critical role in enhancing patient engagement through virtual health assistants and chatbots. These AI tools provide patients with immediate access to information regarding their treatment plans, medication reminders, and even mental health support. By keeping patients informed and engaged in their healthcare process, these technologies empower individuals to take an active role in managing their health, which can lead to better adherence to treatment and improved overall health outcomes.

In conclusion, the implementation of personalized treatment plans through AI not only revolutionizes the healthcare landscape but also enhances the patient experience. With the ability to tailor treatments to individual needs, monitor progress in real-time, and engage patients in their care, AI is paving the way for a future where healthcare is more efficient, effective, and patient-centered. As we continue to harness the power of AI, the potential for improved diagnostics, treatment planning, and overall health management will only expand, promising a brighter future for health and wellness.

AI-Driven Personalized Medicine

AI-Driven Personalized Medicine is at the forefront of transforming healthcare by tailoring treatments and interventions to individual patients based on their unique characteristics. This approach leverages vast amounts of data from various sources, including genetic information, lifestyle factors, and environmental influences, to create a comprehensive profile of each patient. By analyzing these profiles, AI can identify the most effective treatment plans, minimizing the trial-and-error approach often associated with traditional medicine. This shift not only enhances patient outcomes but also optimizes the allocation of healthcare resources.

One of the most significant contributions of AI in personalized medicine is its ability to analyze complex genetic data. Machine learning algorithms can sift through genomic sequences to identify mutations and variations that may predispose individuals to certain diseases or affect their response to specific treatments. This genetic insight allows healthcare providers to recommend personalized therapies, such as targeted drug therapies for cancer patients, which are designed to attack cancer cells based on their genetic makeup. Consequently, patients can experience more effective treatment with fewer side effects, leading to improved quality of life.

In addition to genetic data, AI-driven personalized medicine also incorporates real-time health data from wearable devices and mobile health applications. These tools continuously monitor vital signs, physical activity, and other health metrics, providing a dynamic view of a patient's health status. AI algorithms can analyze this data to detect trends and changes that might indicate a worsening condition or the need for a treatment adjustment. By integrating this real-time data into personalized care plans, healthcare providers can respond proactively to health issues before they escalate, fostering a more preventive approach to healthcare.

Moreover, AI is instrumental in predicting how patients will respond to various treatments based on historical data and clinical trials. Predictive analytics can identify patterns that suggest which treatments are likely to be most effective for specific patient demographics or medical histories. This capability not only enhances the precision of treatment recommendations but also supports shared decision-making between patients and healthcare providers. Patients feel more empowered and engaged in their treatment plans, knowing that their unique needs and circumstances are being considered.

As AI continues to evolve, the future of personalized medicine holds even more promise. Innovations such as advanced imaging analysis and AI-driven drug discovery will further refine treatment options, ensuring that medical interventions are not just effective but also tailored to the individual. The integration of AI in personalized medicine signifies a paradigm shift in healthcare, moving away from a one-size-fits-all approach towards a model that recognizes and respects the uniqueness of each patient, ultimately leading to better health outcomes for all.

The Impact of AI on Clinical Decision-Making

The integration of artificial intelligence (AI) into clinical decision-making is transforming healthcare by enhancing how medical professionals diagnose and treat patients. AI systems leverage vast amounts of data to assist clinicians in making more informed decisions, ultimately leading to improved patient outcomes. By analyzing complex datasets, including medical history, genetic information, and current health trends, AI provides insights that can guide treatment plans and diagnostics, helping healthcare providers to tailor their approach to each individual patient.

AI in diagnostics is particularly significant, as it enables faster and more accurate identification of diseases. Algorithms trained on diverse medical images can detect anomalies that may be missed by the human eye. For instance, AI-powered medical imaging analysis has shown remarkable success in identifying early signs of conditions such as cancer in radiology images, allowing for timely intervention. This technology not only enhances the precision of diagnoses but also reduces the burden on radiologists, allowing them to focus on more complex cases that require nuanced human judgment.

In treatment planning, AI's predictive analytics capabilities are invaluable. By evaluating patterns in patient data, AI can forecast potential health risks and recommend preventive measures. This is particularly beneficial in managing chronic diseases, where ongoing monitoring is crucial. AI-driven personalized medicine takes this a step further by considering individual genetic profiles and lifestyle factors, enabling healthcare providers to customize treatment plans that maximize efficacy and minimize adverse effects. Personalized approaches foster a more proactive stance in patient care, shifting the focus from reactive to preventative health strategies.

AI also plays a critical role in patient monitoring, enhancing how healthcare providers track patients' progress and respond to their needs. With real-time health data analytics, clinicians can monitor vital signs and other health indicators continuously, allowing for immediate intervention if complications arise. Virtual health assistants, powered by AI, further engage patients by providing timely reminders for medication and appointments, along with answering health-related questions. This increases patient compliance and satisfaction, as individuals feel more supported in managing their health.

Lastly, the potential of AI extends to drug discovery and development, where machine learning algorithms can analyze vast datasets to identify promising compounds and predict their effectiveness. This accelerates the process of bringing new treatments to market, ultimately benefiting patients. Automated workflow solutions in hospitals streamline operations, reducing administrative burdens and allowing healthcare professionals to focus more on patient care. As AI continues to evolve, its impact on clinical decision-making will likely expand, fostering a healthcare environment that is not only more efficient but also more responsive to the needs of patients.

Chapter 4: AI for Patient Monitoring

Remote Patient Monitoring Technologies

Remote Patient Monitoring (RPM) technologies represent a significant advancement in the management of healthcare, particularly for individuals requiring ongoing observation and care. By leveraging various digital tools, RPM allows healthcare providers to monitor patients' health metrics in real-time, facilitating proactive interventions.

This technology encompasses a range of devices and applications, including wearables that track vital signs, mobile health applications that gather patient-reported data, and specialized monitoring systems for chronic conditions. The integration of these tools into daily health management practices empowers patients and caregivers alike to take control of health outcomes.

Central to the effectiveness of RPM is its ability to collect vast amounts of health data continuously. This data can be analyzed using artificial intelligence algorithms to identify trends and anomalies that may indicate a change in a patient's condition. For example, AI can analyze heart rate variability captured by smart watches or blood glucose levels logged in mobile apps to alert healthcare providers of potential issues before they escalate. Such predictive capabilities not only enhance the quality of care but also support timely interventions, reducing hospital admissions and improving overall patient satisfaction.

Moreover, RPM technologies facilitate improved communication between patients and healthcare professionals. Through secure messaging platforms and tele-health services, patients can easily share their health data and concerns with their providers. This two-way communication fosters a collaborative approach to care, where patients feel more engaged and informed about their health conditions. Virtual health assistants powered by AI can further enhance this interaction by providing personalized health tips, medication reminders, and answers to common health inquiries, thereby increasing patient adherence to treatment plans.

The role of AI in RPM extends beyond mere data collection and communication. Advanced machine learning algorithms can analyze health data to refine treatment plans tailored to individual patient needs. For instance, AI can identify specific patterns in a patient's response to medication, enabling healthcare providers to make informed adjustments to dosages or explore alternative therapies. This level of personalized medicine ensures that patients receive the most effective treatments based on their unique health profiles, ultimately leading to better health outcomes.

As healthcare continues to evolve with technology, the importance of RPM will only grow. The integration of AI in remote monitoring not only enhances the efficiency of healthcare delivery but also supports public health initiatives, such as predictive analytics for disease outbreaks. The ability to track and analyze health data on a large scale can inform decisions at the community level, contributing to better overall health management strategies. As we look towards the future, the possibilities of RPM technologies in improving diagnostics, treatment planning, and patient engagement are vast, paving the way for a healthier society.

Real-Time Health Data Analytics

Real-time health data analytics is revolutionizing the way individuals manage their health and well-being. By harnessing the power of advanced technologies, healthcare providers can now collect and analyze vast amounts of data in real-time, enabling them to deliver timely insights and interventions. This capability is especially crucial for individuals who are actively involved in their health management, as it empowers them to make informed decisions based on up-to-date information about their conditions and overall health status.

One of the primary benefits of real-time health data analytics is its ability to facilitate proactive health management. Through continuous monitoring of vital signs, lifestyle factors, and environmental conditions, individuals can receive alerts when their health metrics deviate from normal ranges. This immediate feedback allows for timely adjustments to treatment plans or lifestyle changes, ultimately reducing the risk of complications and improving health outcomes. For instance, a person with diabetes can track their blood sugar levels in real time, adjusting their medication or diet as needed, thus maintaining better control over their condition.

Moreover, real-time analytics can enhance patient engagement and adherence to treatment plans. By utilizing mobile applications and wearable devices, individuals can access their health data at any time, enabling them to take an active role in their care. These tools often include features such as personalized reminders for medications or appointments, which are vital in ensuring that patients stay on track with their treatment regimens. Additionally, the integration of chatbots and virtual health assistants can provide immediate support and guidance, answering questions and offering encouragement as patients navigate their health journeys.

The integration of artificial intelligence in real-time health data analytics also plays a significant role in predictive modeling. By analyzing historical data alongside real-time inputs, AI algorithms can identify patterns and predict potential health issues before they arise. This capability is particularly beneficial in managing chronic diseases, where early intervention can significantly alter the disease trajectory. For example, patients at risk of heart disease can be identified through predictive analytics, allowing for personalized prevention strategies that reduce the likelihood of serious events.

As technology continues to evolve, the future of real-time health data analytics holds even more promise. Innovations in machine learning and data science are expected to enhance the accuracy and efficiency of health monitoring tools, making them more accessible to a broader audience. As individuals become more accustomed to using these technologies, the potential for improved health outcomes will grow. By embracing real-time health data analytics, individuals not only take charge of their health but also contribute to a more responsive and personalized healthcare system.

Wearable Devices and AI Integration

Wearable devices have revolutionized the way individuals monitor and manage their health, integrating seamlessly with artificial intelligence to enhance their capabilities. These devices, ranging from smart watches to fitness trackers, collect a wealth of health-related data, including heart rate, activity levels, sleep patterns, and even blood oxygen saturation. By leveraging AI algorithms, this data can be analyzed in real-time, providing users with valuable insights into their health status. This integration not only empowers individuals to take proactive steps towards better health but also enables healthcare providers to access critical information for more informed clinical decisions.

AI integration in wearable devices extends beyond simple data collection; it enables predictive analytics that can forecast potential health issues before they arise. For instance, advanced algorithms can analyze patterns in an individual's daily activity and biometric data to predict heart-related events or other health risks. By alerting users to potential problems early on, wearable devices can facilitate timely interventions, ultimately leading to improved health outcomes. This predictive capability is particularly beneficial for individuals managing chronic conditions, as it allows for more personalized monitoring and timely adjustments to treatment plans.

The use of AI in wearable devices also enhances patient engagement and adherence to health recommendations. Virtual health assistants, powered by AI, can interact with users, providing tailored advice based on their health data. These assistants can remind users to take medications, suggest lifestyle changes, or encourage them to meet their fitness goals. This personalized approach not only fosters a greater sense of accountability but also helps individuals stay motivated in their health journeys. By making health management more accessible and interactive, AI-driven wearable can significantly improve adherence to treatment plans.

Moreover, the integration of AI in wearable devices supports the advancement of personalized medicine. By analyzing individual health data alongside broader population health trends, AI can help identify unique health patterns and risk factors. This information can guide healthcare providers in developing customized treatment plans that align with the specific needs of each patient. As a result, wearable devices equipped with AI technology play a crucial role in the shift towards more individualized healthcare strategies, ensuring that treatments are not only effective but also tailored to the unique characteristics of each person.

In addition to enhancing individual health management, the data collected from wearable devices contributes to broader healthcare research and development efforts. AI can analyze vast amounts of aggregated health data from wearable to identify trends, track disease outbreaks, and improve public health strategies. This capability is particularly valuable in the context of real-time health data analytics, where timely information can inform health policy decisions and resource allocation. As wearable devices continue to evolve and integrate with AI technology, their potential to transform health monitoring, diagnostics, and treatment planning will only expand, paving the way for a healthier future for all.

Chapter 5: Predictive Analytics for Disease Outbreaks

The Power of Predictive Modeling

Predictive modeling has emerged as a transformative force in healthcare, reshaping how we approach diagnostics and treatment. By leveraging historical data, predictive algorithms can identify patterns and trends that inform patient care. This capability allows healthcare providers to anticipate potential health issues before they manifest, enabling proactive management of diseases and improving outcomes. With the integration of artificial intelligence, predictive modeling is becoming increasingly sophisticated, allowing for real-time analysis of vast datasets and providing insights that were previously unattainable.

One of the most significant applications of predictive modeling is in diagnostics. AI algorithms can analyze medical imaging and lab results with remarkable accuracy, identifying early signs of conditions such as cancer or cardiovascular diseases. This early detection is crucial, as it can significantly increase the chances of successful treatment. In addition, predictive models can be employed to assess the risk factors associated with various diseases, helping healthcare professionals to tailor preventive strategies for at-risk populations.

In treatment planning, predictive modeling plays a vital role in personalizing patient care. By examining individual health data, including genetic information and lifestyle factors, AI can recommend the most effective treatment options. This approach not only enhances the efficacy of treatments but also reduces the likelihood of adverse reactions. As healthcare moves toward a more personalized model, the ability to predict how different patients will respond to specific therapies becomes increasingly important.

Moreover, predictive analytics extends beyond individual patient care to broader public health initiatives. By analyzing trends in health data, AI can help predict disease outbreaks, allowing for timely interventions and resource allocation. This capability is particularly crucial in managing infectious diseases, where early warnings can prevent widespread outbreaks and save lives. Additionally, predictive modeling can assist in monitoring chronic diseases, providing insights that can lead to better management strategies and improved quality of life for patients.

As the healthcare landscape continues to evolve with advancements in AI and predictive analytics, the potential for improved patient engagement and outcomes grows. Virtual health assistants powered by AI can provide personalized recommendations and reminders for patients, enhancing adherence to treatment plans. Furthermore, AI-driven tools for mental health support, such as chatbots, can offer immediate assistance and resources for those in need. The power of predictive modeling is not just in its ability to analyze data, but in its capacity to empower individuals to take charge of their health and make informed decisions about their care.

AI in Epidemiology and Public Health

AI in Epidemiology and Public Health is revolutionizing how we understand, predict, and manage health trends on both local and global scales. By harnessing vast amounts of data from various sources, including social media, health records, and environmental data, AI enhances our ability to identify patterns and predict outbreaks of diseases. Predictive analytics powered by AI helps public health officials determine where outbreaks are likely to occur and how they can respond effectively. This proactive approach allows for timely interventions that can save lives and reduce the strain on healthcare systems.

Machine learning algorithms are particularly effective in analyzing complex data sets that would be impractical for human analysts to decipher. These algorithms can sift through historical health data to identify risk factors associated with specific diseases. By understanding these risk factors, public health officials can tailor their prevention strategies and allocate resources more efficiently. For example, AI can help identify populations that are at higher risk for chronic diseases, enabling targeted outreach and education efforts that can lead to better health outcomes.

AI also plays a crucial role in real-time health data analytics, which is essential for monitoring the spread of infectious diseases. With the ability to analyze data from hospitals, laboratories, and even wearable health technology, AI can provide up-to-date information on disease prevalence and patterns. This real-time insight allows health authorities to implement control measures quickly, such as vaccination campaigns or public health advisories. Furthermore, AI systems can predict how diseases might evolve, informing strategies for both prevention and treatment.

Public engagement in health initiatives is also enhanced through AI-driven virtual health assistants and chatbots. These tools can provide personalized health information and support, making it easier for individuals to engage in preventive health measures. By answering questions about symptoms, providing reminders for vaccinations, and offering mental health support, these AI applications empower individuals to take charge of their health. When people feel informed and supported, they are more likely to participate in public health programs and adhere to recommended health behaviors.

The integration of AI in epidemiology and public health not only improves disease surveillance and outbreak response but also fosters a more personalized approach to health management. As AI continues to evolve, its capabilities will expand, leading to innovative solutions that enhance our understanding of health dynamics. The future of public health will increasingly rely on these technologies to address complex health challenges, ultimately leading to healthier communities and improved quality of life for all individuals.

Case Studies of Successful Predictive Analytics

Case studies of successful predictive analytics in healthcare illustrate the transformative potential of AI technologies in enhancing patient care and outcomes. One notable example is the use of predictive analytics in managing chronic diseases, particularly diabetes. Through the analysis of historical patient data, including blood sugar levels, medication adherence, and lifestyle choices, healthcare providers can develop personalized care plans. These plans can predict potential complications, such as diabetic ketoacidosis, allowing for timely interventions that prevent hospitalizations and improve quality of life for patients.

Another compelling case involves the use of predictive models to forecast disease outbreaks. In various regions, public health officials have successfully implemented machine learning algorithms that analyze environmental factors, travel patterns, and historical outbreak data to predict the spread of infectious diseases like influenza and COVID-19. By anticipating surges in cases, healthcare systems can allocate resources more efficiently, implement preventive measures, and engage in targeted public health campaigns, ultimately reducing the burden on healthcare facilities and enhancing community health.

In the realm of cancer treatment, predictive analytics has shown promise in personalizing therapeutic approaches. Data from genomics, patient demographics, and treatment responses can be analyzed to predict which therapies are most likely to succeed for individual patients. For instance, using AI-driven models, oncologists can identify patients who are likely to respond well to immunotherapy, allowing for tailored treatment plans that maximize efficacy while minimizing unnecessary side effects. This approach not only improves patient outcomes but also optimizes healthcare resources by focusing on the most effective treatments.

Additionally, predictive analytics is transforming patient monitoring through wearable technology. Devices that track vital signs and activity levels can feed real-time data into AI systems that analyze this information for early signs of health deterioration. For example, wearable devices monitoring heart rates and rhythms can alert healthcare providers to arrhythmias or other cardiovascular issues before they escalate. This proactive approach to patient monitoring enhances the ability to manage chronic conditions and supports timely medical intervention, significantly improving patient safety and health outcomes.

Finally, the integration of AI-powered virtual health assistants exemplifies the potential for predictive analytics to enhance patient engagement and adherence. These assistants utilize data analytics to provide personalized health advice, medication reminders, and lifestyle recommendations based on individual patient profiles. By predicting potential barriers to adherence and offering tailored support, these virtual tools empower patients to take control of their health, leading to better management of chronic conditions and improved overall health outcomes. The case studies highlight how predictive analytics can not only enhance diagnosis and treatment but also foster a more engaged and informed patient population.

Chapter 6: AI in Drug Discovery and Development

The Drug Development Process

The drug development process is a complex and multifaceted journey that brings potential therapies from the laboratory to the patient's bedside. At its core, this process involves several key stages, including discovery, preclinical testing, clinical trials, and regulatory approval. Each stage is crucial for ensuring that new medications are both effective and safe for human use. With the integration of artificial intelligence in healthcare, these stages are becoming increasingly efficient, allowing for faster and more precise development of new drugs.

During the discovery phase, researchers identify potential drug candidates through various methods, including high-throughput screening and computational modeling. AI plays a pivotal role here by analyzing vast datasets to predict how different compounds may interact with biological targets. Machine learning algorithms can identify patterns that human researchers might miss, significantly speeding up the identification of promising candidates. This capability not only enhances the likelihood of finding effective treatments but also reduces the costs associated with early-stage research.

Once potential drug candidates are identified, they move into preclinical testing. This phase involves laboratory and animal studies to evaluate the safety and biological activity of the compounds. AI can streamline this process by optimizing study designs and analyzing data more efficiently. Predictive analytics can forecast how drugs will behave in humans, helping researchers prioritize which candidates should advance to clinical trials. This approach minimizes the risk of late-stage failures, which can be both financially devastating and detrimental to patient health.

The clinical trial phase is where the efficacy and safety of a drug are tested in human subjects. This stage is traditionally time-consuming and expensive, but AI technologies are transforming the landscape. AI-driven algorithms can optimize patient recruitment by identifying suitable candidates based on genetic, demographic, and health data, ensuring that trials are representative and inclusive. Additionally, real-time data analytics can monitor patient responses more effectively, allowing for quicker adjustments to trial protocols and enhancing overall patient safety.

Finally, after successful clinical trials, drugs must receive regulatory approval before reaching the market. AI can assist in this final phase by streamlining documentation processes and ensuring compliance with regulatory standards. Furthermore, once a drug is on the market, AI continues to play a vital role in post-marketing surveillance, monitoring real-world effectiveness and safety. By harnessing the power of AI throughout the drug development process, healthcare providers can look forward to innovative therapies that are both safer and more personalized, ultimately improving health outcomes for all individuals.

AI's Role in Accelerating Drug Discovery

AI's integration into drug discovery is revolutionizing the pharmaceutical landscape, making the process faster, more efficient, and cost-effective. Traditional drug discovery typically spans several years and involves extensive trial and error, often leading to high failure rates. AI technologies, however, can analyze vast amounts of data swiftly, identifying potential drug candidates and their interactions with biological targets much faster than human researchers. This capability not only shortens the discovery timeline but also enhances the likelihood of success in developing viable therapeutics.

One of the primary ways AI accelerates drug discovery is through machine learning algorithms that can predict the efficacy of new compounds. These algorithms analyze existing datasets, including chemical structures, biological activity, and clinical outcomes, to identify patterns that may not be immediately apparent to human scientists. By leveraging these insights, researchers can prioritize compounds that are more likely to succeed in preclinical and clinical trials, minimizing the time and resources spent on less promising candidates.

Moreover, AI facilitates the identification of new therapeutic targets by analyzing genomic and proteomic data. This is particularly relevant in the context of personalized medicine, where treatments are tailored to individual patients based on their unique genetic profiles. AI systems can uncover correlations between genetic variations and drug responses, enabling the development of targeted therapies that are more effective for specific patient populations. This not only improves patient outcomes but also reduces the incidence of adverse drug reactions, a significant concern in drug therapy.

The collaborative potential of AI extends beyond initial drug discovery. Once a candidate drug is identified, AI can continue to play a vital role throughout the development process. Virtual health assistants can streamline clinical trial management, optimizing patient recruitment and monitoring compliance. Additionally, predictive analytics can help forecast potential obstacles during trials, allowing researchers to adapt their strategies proactively. This continuous feedback loop is essential for ensuring that drug development remains on track and aligned with regulatory requirements.

As the healthcare landscape evolves, the implications of AI in drug discovery are profound. Patients stand to benefit from faster access to innovative treatments that are specifically designed to meet their needs. By harnessing AI's capabilities, the pharmaceutical industry can not only enhance its research and development processes but also improve overall healthcare outcomes. As we move forward, it is crucial for all stakeholders, including patients, healthcare providers, and researchers, to understand and embrace the transformative potential of AI to create a healthier future for everyone.

Case Studies of AI-Driven Drug Development

Case studies of AI-driven drug development illustrate the transformative potential of artificial intelligence in accelerating the discovery and approval of new medications. One notable example is the partnership between pharmaceutical companies and technology firms, which has resulted in the successful application of machine learning algorithms to analyze vast datasets. This collaboration enabled researchers to identify promising drug candidates more efficiently than traditional methods. By leveraging AI's capability to recognize patterns in complex data, companies have significantly reduced the time and resources needed to bring new treatments to market.

Another compelling case study involves the use of AI in repurposing existing drugs for new therapeutic uses. Researchers employed deep learning techniques to analyze extensive biomedical literature and patient data, revealing potential applications for drugs originally designed for different conditions. This innovative approach not only speeds up the drug development process but also minimizes risks, as repurposed drugs have already undergone safety evaluations. The case of a well-known anti-inflammatory drug being repurposed for treating a rare form of cancer highlights how AI can uncover unexpected treatment possibilities.

The integration of AI in preclinical and clinical trial phases has also demonstrated significant advancements. Companies have developed AI models to predict patient responses to specific treatments, enabling more tailored clinical trials. For instance, an AI platform successfully identified patient cohorts likely to respond positively to a novel cancer therapy, leading to a more efficient trial process and improved outcomes. This personalized approach not only enhances the likelihood of success for new drugs but also optimizes resource allocation, making clinical trials more cost-effective.

AI-driven simulations have emerged as a powerful tool in drug development, allowing researchers to model and predict the interactions between potential drugs and biological systems. One case study highlighted a biotech firm that utilized AI to simulate how new compounds would behave in human bodies. By predicting outcomes before actual trials, the company was able to prioritize the most promising candidates, streamlining the development pipeline. This predictive capability is particularly valuable in complex diseases, where traditional trial-and-error methods can be prohibitively slow and expensive.

Finally, the role of AI in enhancing collaboration across various stakeholders in drug development cannot be overlooked. Platforms that utilize AI facilitate information sharing among researchers, clinicians, and regulatory bodies, fostering a more integrated approach to drug discovery. A case study showcasing a network of hospitals and research institutions demonstrated that AI tools enabled real-time data sharing and analysis, accelerating decision-making processes. This collaborative model not only enhances the efficiency of drug development but also promotes innovation by harnessing diverse expertise and resources. Through these case studies, the potential of AI to revolutionize drug development and ultimately improve health outcomes becomes increasingly evident.

Chapter 7: Automated Workflow Solutions for Hospitals

Streamlining Hospital Operations with AI

Streamlining hospital operations with artificial intelligence (AI) is transforming the healthcare landscape, enhancing efficiency and improving patient outcomes. Hospitals face a myriad of challenges, including high operational costs, increasing patient volumes, and the need for more effective resource management. By integrating AI technologies, healthcare facilities can automate routine tasks, optimize workflows, and allocate resources more effectively. This not only reduces the burden on healthcare professionals but also allows them to focus on providing high-quality patient care.

One significant area where AI is making an impact is in patient scheduling and management. Traditional methods of appointment booking can lead to overbooking or underutilization of resources. AI-driven systems can analyze patient data and historical trends to predict demand, optimizing schedules to ensure that healthcare providers are available when needed. This predictive capability minimizes wait times for patients, enhances the patient experience, and maximizes the use of hospital facilities, leading to better operational efficiency.

AI is also playing a crucial role in medical imaging analysis. Advanced algorithms can process images faster and with greater accuracy than human radiologists, identifying potential health issues that may be overlooked. This capability not only speeds up the diagnostic process but also reduces the likelihood of human error. Hospitals adopting AI-powered imaging solutions can improve their diagnostic accuracy and provide timely interventions, which is essential for effective treatment planning and improved patient outcomes.

Moreover, AI enhances real-time health data analytics, allowing hospitals to monitor patient conditions continuously. By integrating wearable technology and electronic health records, AI systems can analyze vast amounts of data to provide actionable insights. This enables healthcare providers to identify early signs of deterioration in patients, ensuring timely interventions. Such proactive monitoring is particularly beneficial for managing chronic conditions, where early detection can significantly alter treatment trajectories and improve quality of life for patients.

Finally, AI-driven automated workflow solutions streamline administrative tasks such as billing, reporting, and compliance management. These systems reduce the administrative burden on healthcare staff, allowing them to focus more on patient care rather than paperwork. As hospitals increasingly adopt these technologies, they are likely to see a reduction in operational costs and an improvement in overall service delivery. By leveraging AI in these ways, healthcare facilities can not only enhance their operational efficiency but also create a more patient-centered environment that ultimately leads to better health outcomes for all.

AI in Resource Allocation and Management

AI is revolutionizing resource allocation and management in healthcare, leading to more efficient use of resources and improved patient outcomes. By leveraging vast amounts of data, AI systems can identify patterns and predict needs, allowing healthcare providers to allocate resources where they are most needed. For instance, predictive analytics can help hospitals anticipate patient admissions during peak seasons, ensuring that staff and facilities are adequately prepared. This proactive approach minimizes overcrowding, reduces wait times, and enhances the overall patient experience.

In treatment planning, AI can optimize resource use by analyzing patient data and treatment outcomes. By integrating various health metrics, AI systems can recommend personalized treatment plans that consider both clinical effectiveness and resource availability. This ensures that patients receive the most appropriate care without overwhelming the healthcare system. Moreover, machine learning algorithms can identify which treatments yield the best results for specific patient populations, further refining resource allocation strategies.

AI's role in patient monitoring also contributes significantly to efficient resource management. Continuous monitoring through wearable devices and AI-driven applications allows for real-time health data analytics, enabling providers to closely track patient progress. This data can signal when a patient requires immediate attention, allowing healthcare professionals to prioritize their resources effectively. Additionally, AI can help in identifying at-risk patients earlier, facilitating timely interventions that can prevent more severe health issues down the line.

The integration of AI in automated workflow solutions has transformed hospital operations, streamlining processes and reducing administrative burdens. By automating routine tasks such as scheduling, billing, and patient follow-up, healthcare staff can focus more on patient care rather than paperwork. These solutions not only enhance efficiency but also lead to cost savings, which can be redirected toward improving patient services or investing in advanced technologies. This holistic improvement in management fosters a more responsive healthcare environment.

Finally, AI-driven personalized medicine offers significant potential in optimizing resource allocation. By tailoring treatments to individual genetic profiles and health conditions, healthcare providers can minimize unnecessary interventions and focus on the most effective therapies. This precision not only improves patient outcomes but also conserves resources, reducing waste and ensuring that healthcare systems can operate sustainably. As AI continues to evolve, its impact on resource allocation and management will be critical in shaping the future of healthcare, enhancing both efficiency and quality of care for all individuals.

Improving Patient Flow and Reducing Wait Times

Improving patient flow and reducing wait times in healthcare settings is crucial for enhancing the overall patient experience and outcomes. With the integration of artificial intelligence, healthcare providers can streamline processes that traditionally caused delays. AI technologies can analyze patient data in real-time, allowing staff to prioritize cases based on urgency and complexity. This means that patients who need immediate care can receive it faster, while those with less critical needs can be appropriately scheduled, alleviating congestion in waiting areas.

One of the significant advancements in AI is the development of predictive analytics, which can forecast patient volumes and identify peak times for specific services. By utilizing historical data and trends, healthcare facilities can optimize staffing levels and resource allocation. This proactive approach allows for better management of patient flow, reducing bottlenecks that typically lead to long wait times. For instance, hospitals can anticipate increased demand during flu seasons and adjust their operations accordingly, ensuring that patients are seen in a timely manner.

AI-powered virtual health assistants play a vital role in patient engagement and pre-visit triage. These intelligent systems can interact with patients via chatbots and mobile applications, helping them understand their symptoms and directing them to the appropriate care paths. By addressing common questions and concerns before patients even arrive at a facility, these AI solutions can significantly reduce the number of unnecessary visits and streamline the check-in process. This not only enhances patient satisfaction but also improves the efficiency of healthcare providers.

Real-time health data analytics is another transformative tool for improving patient flow. By continuously monitoring patient conditions and operational metrics, healthcare providers can respond swiftly to emerging challenges. For example, if a particular department is experiencing an influx of patients, AI systems can alert management to redistribute staff or resources effectively. This dynamic approach ensures that healthcare facilities are not only reactive but also proactive in maintaining optimal patient flow.

Ultimately, the integration of AI in healthcare settings leads to a more efficient, responsive, and patient-centered approach to care. By leveraging these technologies, providers can reduce wait times, enhance operational efficiency, and improve the overall experience for patients. As the healthcare landscape continues to evolve, embracing AI solutions will be essential in achieving a future where timely access to care is the norm, not the exception.

Chapter 8: Virtual Health Assistants for Patient Engagement

The Rise of Chatbots and Virtual Assistants

The emergence of chatbots and virtual assistants has revolutionized various sectors, including healthcare. These AI-driven tools are designed to enhance patient engagement, streamline communication, and provide immediate support. Their rise can be attributed to the growing demand for efficient healthcare solutions that cater to the needs of both patients and providers. As individuals increasingly seek personalized and accessible health information, chatbots have become invaluable in bridging the gap between patients and healthcare professionals.

In diagnostics, chatbots play a crucial role in guiding patients through symptom assessment and preliminary evaluations. By using natural language processing, these virtual assistants can interact with users in real-time, helping them identify potential health issues based on their symptoms. This immediate support not only empowers patients to seek timely medical advice but also alleviates the pressure on healthcare systems by filtering out non-urgent cases. Consequently, practitioners can focus their attention on patients who require more complex care.

As treatment planning evolves, virtual assistants can assist healthcare providers by offering evidence-based recommendations tailored to individual patient profiles. Through the integration of machine learning algorithms, these tools can analyze vast amounts of patient data, including medical history and genetic information, to propose personalized treatment plans. This capability not only enhances the precision of treatment but also fosters a more collaborative approach between patients and healthcare professionals, ensuring that patients are actively involved in their care decisions.

Patient monitoring has also seen significant advancements through the use of chatbots and virtual assistants. By facilitating continuous communication between patients and their healthcare teams, these technologies can track patient progress, medication adherence, and overall health metrics. This real-time data collection enables healthcare providers to make informed decisions and adjust treatment plans as necessary. Furthermore, AI-powered virtual assistants can remind patients about appointments and medications, thereby improving overall compliance and health outcomes.

In areas such as mental health support, chatbots provide a vital resource for individuals seeking immediate assistance. By offering a non-judgmental space for users to express their feelings and concerns, these virtual assistants can guide them through coping strategies and recommend professional help when needed. The accessibility of chatbots ensures that support is available around the clock, making mental health resources more attainable for those in need. As the integration of AI in healthcare continues to expand, the role of chatbots and virtual assistants will undoubtedly grow, further enhancing the quality and accessibility of health services for all.

Enhancing Patient Communication and Support

Enhancing patient communication and support is becoming increasingly vital in the evolving landscape of healthcare, particularly with the integration of artificial intelligence. By leveraging AI technologies, healthcare providers can foster better communication with patients, ensuring that individuals feel heard, valued, and supported throughout their health journeys. This enhanced communication is not only about conveying medical information but also about building trust and understanding between patients and healthcare professionals.

AI-powered virtual health assistants are revolutionizing patient engagement by providing timely information and support. These digital tools can answer questions, schedule appointments, and offer reminders for medication, allowing patients to manage their health with greater ease. By being accessible 24/7, virtual assistants can provide immediate responses to patient inquiries, reducing anxiety and empowering patients to take control of their health. This continuous support fosters a proactive approach to healthcare, where patients are encouraged to actively participate in their treatment plans.

Moreover, predictive analytics can play a substantial role in enhancing patient communication. By analyzing data trends and patterns, AI can help healthcare providers anticipate potential health issues before they arise. This proactive approach allows for timely interventions and facilitates open discussions between patients and providers regarding their health risks. When patients are equipped with information about potential health challenges, they can engage more thoughtfully in conversations about preventive measures and treatment options.

Additionally, AI-driven personalized medicine ensures that treatment plans are tailored to the unique needs of each patient. By analyzing genetic information and health histories, AI can suggest individualized therapies that are more likely to be effective. This personalization not only improves treatment outcomes but also allows for more meaningful communication between patients and their healthcare teams. When patients understand that their treatment plans are specifically designed for them, they are more likely to engage in discussions about their care and express their preferences and concerns.

Finally, the integration of chatbots for mental health support exemplifies how AI can enhance communication and provide essential support to patients facing emotional challenges. These chatbots can offer immediate assistance, providing coping strategies and resources for individuals in need. By ensuring that mental health support is readily available, patients can feel more comfortable discussing their mental well-being with healthcare professionals. This open dialogue is crucial in creating a supportive environment where patients can share their experiences and seek help without stigma. As AI continues to evolve, its role in enhancing patient communication and support will undoubtedly expand, leading to improved health outcomes and a more engaged patient population.

Studies of Successful Implementations

The integration of artificial intelligence in healthcare has led to numerous successful implementations that significantly enhance diagnostic and treatment processes. One notable case is the use of AI-powered medical imaging analysis in radiology. Hospitals that have adopted AI algorithms to interpret imaging data, such as X-rays and MRIs, report a marked increase in diagnostic accuracy and efficiency. For instance, a leading hospital utilized an AI system to analyze breast cancer screenings, resulting in a 20% reduction in false positives and a 15% increase in early detection rates. This case underscores the potential of AI to not only augment the capabilities of healthcare professionals but also to improve patient outcomes.

Another compelling example can be found in predictive analytics for disease outbreaks. During a recent flu season, one health organization employed machine learning algorithms to analyze historical patient data and social media trends. This approach enabled them to predict flu outbreak patterns in real-time, allowing for timely public health interventions and resource allocation. As a result, affected communities received vaccinations and educational materials earlier, leading to a significant decrease in flu-related hospitalizations. This case highlights how AI can play a critical role in proactive health management and prevention strategies.

AI-driven personalized medicine is another area where successful implementations have emerged. A prominent cancer treatment center has developed a platform that uses genetic profiling to tailor treatment plans to individual patients. By analyzing genetic markers and treatment responses from vast datasets, the AI system recommends personalized therapies that are more likely to succeed based on a patient's unique genetic makeup. This approach has led to improved treatment outcomes and reduced side effects, demonstrating the effectiveness of AI in creating customized healthcare solutions.

The rise of virtual health assistants has also proven beneficial in enhancing patient engagement. A healthcare provider launched a chatbot designed to assist patients with medication adherence and appointment reminders. This AI-driven assistant utilizes natural language processing to interact with patients, answer their questions, and provide personalized health tips. The implementation resulted in a significant increase in patient engagement, with reported adherence rates for chronic disease management rising by 30%. This case exemplifies how AI can simplify healthcare processes and foster better communication between patients and providers.

Lastly, automated workflow solutions for hospitals have revolutionized operational efficiency. A large hospital network implemented an AI system to streamline administrative tasks, such as patient scheduling and billing. By automating these processes, the hospital reduced waiting times and improved patient satisfaction scores. Additionally, staff were able to focus more on direct patient care rather than administrative burdens. This case illustrates the broader impact of AI on healthcare systems, enabling providers to deliver higher quality care while optimizing their operational capabilities.

Chapter 9: Machine Learning for Genetic Disorder Identification

Understanding Genetic Disorders

Genetic disorders arise from anomalies in an individual's DNA, which can lead to a range of health issues, from mild to severe. These disorders can be inherited from one or both parents or can occur spontaneously due to mutations. Understanding the complexities of genetic disorders is essential for effective diagnosis and treatment planning. With advancements in genomic research, we have gained insights into how specific genes contribute to various conditions, making it possible to identify at-risk individuals and tailor health strategies accordingly.

Artificial intelligence plays a pivotal role in the identification and analysis of genetic disorders. Machine learning algorithms can process vast amounts of genetic data, allowing for the detection of patterns that may indicate the presence of a disorder. These technologies enhance traditional diagnostic methods by providing more accurate and timely results. For families with a history of genetic disorders, AI can help identify carriers of genetic mutations and facilitate early interventions, thereby improving outcomes for individuals at risk.

In terms of treatment planning, AI-driven personalized medicine is transforming how healthcare providers approach genetic disorders. By analyzing a patient's genetic profile, AI can recommend targeted therapies that are more likely to be effective based on the individual's unique genetic makeup. This tailored approach not only enhances the efficacy of treatments but also minimizes side effects, as therapies can be chosen based on how a patient's body is genetically predisposed to respond to certain medications.

Patient monitoring has also benefited from AI innovations, particularly for those with chronic genetic conditions. Real-time health data analytics can track a patient's vital signs and symptoms through wearable devices, ensuring that any deviations from the norm are promptly addressed. AI-powered virtual health assistants can engage with patients to provide reminders for medication, schedule follow-ups, and offer support, creating a comprehensive care network that emphasizes proactive health management.

Finally, the integration of AI in drug discovery and development has accelerated the process of finding new treatments for genetic disorders. By predicting how different compounds might interact with specific genetic profiles, researchers can streamline the development of new therapies. This not only shortens the time frame for bringing effective drugs to market but also enhances the likelihood that these treatments will be beneficial for patients with genetic conditions. As these technologies continue to evolve, they promise to reshape the landscape of healthcare, making it possible for individuals to manage their health in more informed and effective ways.

The Role of Machine Learning in Genetics

The integration of machine learning in genetics represents a significant advancement in how we understand and treat various health conditions. This technology facilitates the analysis of vast amounts of genetic data, enabling researchers and healthcare providers to identify patterns that would be impossible to discern through traditional methods. By leveraging algorithms that can learn from and make predictions based on complex datasets, machine learning enhances our ability to diagnose genetic disorders more accurately and rapidly. This capability is particularly crucial in settings where timely intervention can make a substantial difference in patient outcomes.

Machine learning algorithms can process genomic sequences and pinpoint anomalies that may indicate genetic disorders. Techniques such as deep learning are employed to analyze high-dimensional data, such as whole-genome sequencing, which can reveal mutations associated with hereditary diseases. This level of analysis allows for earlier detection of conditions, leading to proactive management strategies tailored to individual patients. Consequently, machine learning not only aids in identifying existing genetic disorders but also plays a vital role in predicting potential health risks based on a person's genetic profile.

In addition to diagnosis, machine learning has transformed the landscape of personalized medicine. By integrating genetic data with other health information, such as lifestyle factors and environmental influences, healthcare providers can develop customized treatment plans that cater to the unique genetic makeup of each patient. This approach increases the efficacy of treatments and minimizes adverse reactions, as therapies can be tailored to work with a patient's specific genetic characteristics. As machine learning continues to evolve, its ability to enhance personalized medicine will likely lead to more effective interventions across a broader range of conditions.

Moreover, the role of machine learning extends to drug discovery and development. By analyzing genetic data, researchers can identify potential drug targets and predict how different genetic profiles will respond to specific therapies. This not only accelerates the development of new medications but also ensures that they are more effective for the populations who need them most. The synergy between machine learning and genetics thus holds the potential to revolutionize the pharmaceutical industry, leading to faster, safer, and more targeted treatments.

Finally, the implications of machine learning in genetics are far-reaching for patient engagement and monitoring. Virtual health assistants powered by AI can provide patients with insights into their genetic predispositions, encouraging them to take proactive steps in managing their health. By understanding their genetic risks, individuals can better engage in preventive health behaviors and adhere to personalized treatment plans. This not only empowers patients but also fosters a more collaborative relationship between healthcare providers and those they serve, ultimately contributing to improved health outcomes across diverse populations.

Future Directions in Genetic Research

The future of genetic research is poised to revolutionize healthcare, particularly in the realms of diagnostics and treatment planning. As artificial intelligence continues to evolve, its integration into genetic research is expected to enhance our understanding of complex genetic disorders and facilitate the development of targeted therapies. With AI's ability to analyze vast datasets quickly and accurately, researchers can identify genetic markers associated with various diseases, leading to earlier diagnosis and more effective treatment strategies. This capability is particularly crucial as we move towards a more personalized approach in medicine, where treatments can be tailored to the unique genetic makeup of each patient.

One significant direction in genetic research is the application of machine learning algorithms to genomic data. These algorithms can sift through enormous amounts of genetic information to uncover patterns and associations that may not be evident to human researchers. By employing AI in this manner, scientists can enhance their ability to identify genetic disorders and predict disease susceptibility. This not only aids in proactive health management but also empowers individuals to make informed decisions about their health based on their genetic predispositions. As a result, we can expect a shift towards preventive healthcare, where genetic insights guide lifestyle choices and early interventions.

Another promising avenue is the use of AI in drug discovery and development. Genetic research plays a critical role in understanding how different individuals respond to medications based on their genetic profiles. AI-powered platforms can analyze genetic data alongside clinical trial results to identify which drug formulations are likely to be the most effective for specific genetic variants. This approach not only accelerates the drug development process but also minimizes the risk of adverse effects, leading to safer and more effective treatments for patients. As pharmaceutical companies increasingly adopt these technologies, we can anticipate a new era of precision medicine that is more aligned with the genetic needs of diverse populations.

Patient monitoring and engagement are also set to benefit from advancements in genetic research facilitated by AI. Virtual health assistants equipped with genetic insights can provide personalized recommendations to patients, enhancing their understanding of their health conditions and treatment options. By integrating genetic data with real-time health analytics, these AI-driven tools can alert patients and healthcare providers to potential health risks before they become critical. This proactive approach not only improves patient outcomes but also fosters a more engaged and informed patient population, ultimately leading to better adherence to treatment plans. Finally, collaborative efforts between researchers, healthcare providers, and technology developers will be essential in shaping the future of genetic research. Establishing robust data-sharing frameworks and ethical guidelines will ensure that genetic information is used responsibly and effectively. As AI continues to enhance our capabilities in genetic research, it is vital to maintain a focus on the human aspects of healthcare, ensuring that advancements contribute positively to patient care. By leveraging the power of AI in genetic research, we can expect a future where health management is more precise, personalized, and proactive, improving the quality of life for individuals everywhere.

Chapter 10: Chat bots for Mental Health Support

The Importance of Mental Health Care

Mental health care is a crucial component of overall health that often receives less attention than physical health. As society becomes more aware of the importance of mental well-being, the role of mental health care must be emphasized, particularly in the context of advancements in artificial intelligence (AI). AI technologies are transforming how mental health services are delivered, making them more accessible, efficient, and tailored to individual needs. This evolution is essential, as mental health issues affect millions of people worldwide, and timely intervention can significantly improve quality of life.

AI-powered tools, such as chatbots and virtual health assistants, are increasingly being utilized to provide mental health support. These technologies can engage with individuals, offering immediate assistance and resources for those experiencing anxiety, depression, or other mental health challenges. By leveraging natural language processing and machine learning, these systems can provide personalized responses and interventions, helping users navigate their feelings and access appropriate care. This accessibility can bridge the gap for those who may hesitate to seek help due to stigma or logistical barriers.

In addition to direct support, AI plays a pivotal role in diagnostics and treatment planning for mental health conditions. AI algorithms can analyze vast amounts of patient data to identify patterns and predict outcomes, allowing healthcare providers to make informed decisions. For example, machine learning models can assess genetic, behavioral, and environmental factors to determine the most effective treatment options for individuals with mental health disorders. This data-driven approach enhances the precision of mental health care, ensuring that patients receive tailored interventions that address their unique circumstances.

Predictive analytics also contributes to mental health care by facilitating early intervention strategies. By analyzing trends in health data, AI can identify potential outbreaks of mental health issues within specific populations or communities. This proactive approach allows healthcare providers to implement preventive measures, reducing the incidence of severe mental health crises. Moreover, real-time health data analytics can monitor patients' progress, enabling clinicians to adjust treatment plans as needed and ensuring that care remains effective throughout the recovery process.

As we embrace the future of health, the integration of AI into mental health care represents a significant advancement in how we understand and treat psychological conditions. The importance of mental health cannot be overstated, and with the help of AI technologies, we can create a more supportive environment for individuals seeking help. By prioritizing mental health care alongside physical health, we can foster a holistic approach to wellness that acknowledges the interconnectedness of mind and body, ultimately leading to healthier individuals and communities.

AI-Powered Chatbots in Mental Health

AI-powered chatbots are emerging as valuable tools in the field of mental health, providing support and resources to individuals seeking help. These digital assistants are designed to engage users in conversations, offering immediate responses to queries and concerns related to mental well-being. By leveraging natural language processing and machine learning algorithms, chatbots can understand and interpret user input, allowing for more personalized interactions. This capability enables chatbots to deliver tailored advice, coping strategies, and resources, making mental health support more accessible to a broader audience.

One significant advantage of AI-powered chatbots is their ability to provide immediate support at any time. Unlike traditional therapy sessions, which may require scheduling and travel, chatbots are available 24/7, allowing users to seek help whenever they need it. This immediacy can be especially beneficial during moments of crisis or when individuals feel uncomfortable seeking help from a human therapist. Through real-time interaction, chatbots can help users navigate their emotions, offering prompt reassurance and guidance that can alleviate feelings of anxiety or distress.

Moreover, these chatbots can serve as a bridge to professional mental health services. By identifying users who may be in need of further assistance, chatbots can recommend appropriate resources, such as hotlines, support groups, or professional therapy options. This proactive approach not only raises awareness of available mental health services but also helps to reduce the stigma associated with seeking help. Users who might hesitate to reach out for human assistance can feel more comfortable engaging with a chatbot, allowing them to take the first step towards recovery.

The application of AI in mental health chatbots also extends to data collection and analysis. By monitoring user interactions, chatbots can gather valuable insights into mental health trends and common concerns. This information can be instrumental for healthcare professionals and researchers aiming to understand the mental health landscape better. Additionally, the data can inform the development of more effective therapeutic strategies and interventions, ultimately enhancing the quality of mental health care.

As AI technology continues to evolve, the potential for chatbots in mental health support will only grow. Future advancements may lead to even more sophisticated interactions, including the ability to recognize and respond to users' emotional states through voice tone or text sentiment analysis. By integrating these capabilities, chatbots could provide a more empathetic and supportive experience. As we move forward, embracing AI-powered chatbots in mental health care represents a significant step towards a more inclusive and responsive healthcare system, empowering individuals to take charge of their mental well-being.

Evaluating Effectiveness and Patient Engagement

Evaluating the effectiveness of AI in healthcare is crucial for ensuring that patients receive optimal care. As AI technologies become increasingly integrated into diagnostics, treatment planning, and patient monitoring, it is important to assess their impact on patient outcomes. Effectiveness can be measured through various indicators, including accuracy of diagnoses, speed of treatment initiation, and overall patient satisfaction. By analyzing these metrics, healthcare providers can determine which AI applications are delivering real benefits and which may require further refinement.

Patient engagement is another vital component in evaluating AI's role in healthcare. Engaged patients are more likely to adhere to treatment plans, communicate openly with healthcare providers, and participate actively in their health management. AI-driven tools, such as virtual health assistants and chatbots, are designed to facilitate this engagement by providing timely information and support. These technologies can help patients navigate their healthcare journeys, answer common questions, and remind them of important tasks, such as medication adherence or upcoming appointments.

One effective way to assess patient engagement is through feedback mechanisms that capture the patient experience with AI tools. Surveys and interviews can provide insights into how patients perceive these technologies and their perceived value in managing their health. Additionally, data analytics can track usage patterns of AI applications, allowing healthcare providers to identify areas where engagement may be lacking and make necessary adjustments to improve user experience.

Moreover, the integration of predictive analytics allows for proactive engagement strategies that can enhance patient involvement in their care. By leveraging data from a variety of sources, healthcare providers can anticipate patient needs and tailor interventions accordingly. This not only improves patient engagement but also fosters a more personalized approach to treatment, aligning with the growing trend of personalized medicine. When patients feel that their specific needs are being addressed, they are more likely to stay engaged and committed to their health goals.

As healthcare continues to evolve with the integration of AI, ongoing evaluation of effectiveness and patient engagement will be essential. By continuously monitoring the impact of these technologies on health outcomes and patient experiences, healthcare providers can make informed decisions about adopting new AI solutions and refining existing ones. The ultimate goal is to create a healthcare environment where technology enhances the patient experience, leading to better health outcomes and a more empowered patient population.

Chapter 11: AI-Enhanced Rehabilitation Programs

The Role of AI in Physical Rehabilitation

The integration of artificial intelligence in physical rehabilitation represents a significant advancement in healthcare, transforming how patients recover from injuries and surgeries. AI technologies are increasingly being utilized to create personalized rehabilitation programs that take into account an individual's unique needs, capabilities, and progress. By analyzing data from various sources, including medical history, physical assessments, and real-time performance metrics, AI systems can develop tailored exercise regimens that optimize recovery and enhance overall outcomes.

AI-powered tools also play a crucial role in monitoring patients during their rehabilitation journey. Wearable devices equipped with sensors can track a patient's movements, providing valuable feedback on their performance. This data is analyzed by AI algorithms, which can identify patterns and suggest modifications to the rehabilitation plan. This dynamic approach not only keeps patients engaged but also minimizes the risk of re-injury by ensuring that exercises are performed correctly and at appropriate intensity levels.

Furthermore, AI enhances the effectiveness of rehabilitation through virtual health assistants that guide patients throughout their recovery process. These assistants can provide reminders for exercises, answer questions about rehabilitation techniques, and offer motivational support. By maintaining a constant line of communication, these AI-driven tools foster a sense of accountability and encourage adherence to rehabilitation programs, which is often a challenge in traditional settings.

The predictive analytics capabilities of AI can also be beneficial in physical rehabilitation. By analyzing historical data from similar patient cases, AI can forecast potential recovery trajectories and identify patients who may require additional support. This proactive approach allows healthcare providers to intervene early, ensuring that patients do not plateau in their recovery and that appropriate adjustments are made to their rehabilitation plans as needed.

Ultimately, the role of AI in physical rehabilitation is about enhancing patient outcomes and streamlining the recovery process. As technology continues to evolve, the integration of AI in this field is likely to expand further, offering innovative solutions that empower patients and healthcare providers alike. By leveraging the power of AI, the future of physical rehabilitation promises to be more efficient, personalized, and effective, paving the way for healthier lives.

Personalized Rehabilitation Plans through AI

Personalized rehabilitation plans powered by artificial intelligence represent a significant advancement in the way health care providers approach recovery for individuals. Traditional rehabilitation programs often adopt a one-size-fits-all methodology, which may not adequately address the unique needs of each patient. With the integration of AI, rehabilitation can be tailored to the specific requirements of patients, taking into consideration individual health data, recovery goals, and personal circumstances. This customization enhances the effectiveness of rehabilitation efforts, potentially leading to better outcomes and a faster return to health.

AI algorithms can analyze vast amounts of data from various sources, including medical history, genetic predispositions, and real-time health metrics. By leveraging machine learning, these algorithms can identify patterns and predict the most effective rehabilitation strategies for each patient. For instance, if a patient has a history of knee injuries, the AI can suggest a rehabilitation plan that incorporates targeted exercises to strengthen the knee while avoiding movements that could exacerbate the condition. This data-driven approach ensures that rehabilitation is not only personalized but also grounded in evidence-based practices.

Furthermore, AI enhances patient monitoring during rehabilitation. Wearable devices and mobile applications can track a patient's progress in real time, providing valuable feedback to both the patient and healthcare providers. This continuous monitoring allows for dynamic adjustments to the rehabilitation plan as needed. If a patient is progressing slower than expected, the AI can recommend modifications to the regimen, such as increased frequency of therapy sessions or changes in exercise intensity. This responsiveness can help prevent setbacks and keep patients engaged in their recovery journey.

The role of virtual health assistants also comes into play, offering support and encouragement throughout the rehabilitation process. These AI-driven tools can provide patients with reminders for exercises, tips for pain management, and motivational messages to maintain their commitment to recovery. By fostering an interactive and supportive environment, virtual health assistants promote higher levels of patient engagement, which is crucial for the success of rehabilitation efforts. These tools can also facilitate communication between patients and healthcare providers, ensuring that any concerns are promptly addressed.

As we look toward the future, the integration of AI in rehabilitation not only improves individual patient outcomes but also has broader implications for healthcare systems. By streamlining rehabilitation processes and enhancing the precision of treatment plans, AI can lead to reduced healthcare costs and improved resource allocation. Ultimately, personalized rehabilitation plans through AI signify a transformative shift in healthcare, empowering patients to take an active role in their recovery while ensuring that they receive the most effective care tailored to their unique needs.

Future Innovations in Rehabilitation Technology

Future innovations in rehabilitation technology are poised to transform the landscape of patient recovery and support. As artificial intelligence continues to permeate various sectors of healthcare, rehabilitation services are increasingly integrating these advancements to enhance patient outcomes. From personalized recovery plans to real-time monitoring, the intersection of AI and rehabilitation technology offers a promising future where recovery can be more efficient, effective, and tailored to individual needs.

One of the significant advancements in rehabilitation technology is the development of AI-driven personalized rehabilitation programs. These programs leverage machine learning algorithms to analyze a patient's unique health data, physical capabilities, and recovery goals. By continuously assessing progress and adjusting therapy protocols in real-time, these systems ensure that patients receive the most appropriate exercises and interventions throughout their recovery journey. This level of customization not only improves patient engagement but can also lead to faster and more effective rehabilitation outcomes.

In addition to personalized programs, virtual health assistants are set to play a vital role in rehabilitation. These AI-powered tools can provide patients with on-demand support, answering questions about their recovery process and offering reminders for exercises or medications. By facilitating constant communication between patients and healthcare providers, virtual assistants can help in monitoring adherence to rehabilitation protocols. This can significantly reduce the risk of complications and enhance the overall recovery experience, making rehabilitation more accessible and manageable for individuals.

Real-time health data analytics also represents a critical innovation in rehabilitation technology. By collecting and analyzing data from wearable devices and mobile applications, healthcare providers can gain insights into a patient's daily activities, pain levels, and physical performance. This information allows for timely interventions and adjustments to rehabilitation plans based on a patient's current condition. Furthermore, predictive analytics can forecast potential setbacks in recovery, enabling proactive measures that can prevent complications and ensure a smoother healing process.

Finally, the integration of AI in rehabilitation is fostering the development of immersive therapies, such as virtual reality (VR) and augmented reality (AR). These technologies can create engaging, interactive environments for patients to practice movements and improve mobility in a safe and controlled setting. By simulating real-life scenarios, patients can gain confidence in their abilities and overcome psychological barriers that often accompany rehabilitation. As these innovations continue to evolve, the future of rehabilitation technology promises to enhance not only physical recovery but also the emotional and psychological well-being of patients.

Chapter 12: Ethical Considerations in AI Healthcare

Data Privacy and Patient Consent

In the rapidly evolving landscape of healthcare, the integration of artificial intelligence (AI) brings forth significant advancements in diagnostics, treatment planning, and patient monitoring. However, this evolution is accompanied by profound considerations regarding data privacy and patient consent. As healthcare providers leverage AI technologies to enhance patient care, the protection of sensitive health information becomes paramount. Patients must be assured that their personal data is handled with the utmost care and integrity, which necessitates a thorough understanding of how AI systems utilize this information.

Patient consent is a fundamental component of ethical healthcare practices. In the context of AI, it extends beyond mere agreement; it involves informing patients about how their data will be collected, used, and shared. This transparency is crucial, especially when AI algorithms analyze vast amounts of health data for diagnostics and treatment planning. Patients should be equipped with clear information about the purpose of data collection, the potential benefits of AI-driven approaches, and their rights regarding their own health information. Ensuring informed consent helps build trust between patients and healthcare providers, which is essential for the successful implementation of AI technologies?

Moreover, as AI systems become more sophisticated, the risk of data breaches and misuse of personal health information increases. Healthcare organizations must prioritize robust data security measures to protect against unauthorized access and potential exploitation. This includes employing advanced encryption methods, implementing strict access controls, and conducting regular audits of data usage. By establishing strong safeguards, healthcare providers can enhance patient confidence in AI technologies, assuring them that their health data is secure and used solely for their benefit. The relationship between AI and patient consent is also influenced by the concept of data ownership. Patients increasingly seek control over their health information, advocating for the right to dictate how their data is used. This shift necessitates a reevaluation of traditional consent models to accommodate the dynamic nature of AI applications. Healthcare providers must engage patients in discussions about data sharing and usage, empowering them to make informed choices about their own health information. Such collaborative approaches can foster a more ethical and patient-centered healthcare environment.

As the healthcare sector continues to embrace AI, the dialogue surrounding data privacy and patient consent will remain critical. Stakeholders, including healthcare providers, technology developers, and regulatory bodies, must work together to establish comprehensive guidelines and policies that protect patient rights while promoting innovation. By prioritizing data privacy and informed consent, the integration of AI in healthcare can lead to enhanced diagnostics, improved treatment outcomes, and ultimately, a more efficient and trustworthy healthcare system that benefits all individuals.

Addressing Bias in AI Algorithms

Bias in AI algorithms poses a significant challenge in the healthcare sector, potentially leading to disparities in diagnostics, treatment, and patient outcomes. As AI technologies increasingly play a role in healthcare decision-making, it becomes crucial to recognize and mitigate biases that can arise from the data used to train these algorithms. Bias can manifest in various forms, including racial, gender, and socioeconomic disparities, which can affect the accuracy and effectiveness of AI-driven solutions. Addressing these biases is essential to ensure equitable access to healthcare for all individuals, regardless of their background.

The initial step in addressing bias is to ensure diverse and representative datasets are utilized in the training of AI algorithms. Many existing datasets may under represent certain populations, leading to algorithms that perform well for some groups while failing for others. For instance, if a diagnostic algorithm is trained predominantly on data from a specific demographic, it may not accurately identify conditions in patients from different backgrounds. By curating datasets that reflect a wide range of demographics, healthcare providers can develop AI systems that are more reliable and inclusive. Moreover, transparency in the development and deployment of AI algorithms is critical. Stakeholders, including healthcare professionals, developers, and patients, should be informed about how algorithms are created and the data that underpin them. This transparency enables greater scrutiny of the decision-making processes and helps to identify potential biases early in the development phase. Regular audits and evaluations of AI systems can further ensure that any biases are detected and corrected, promoting trust in AI applications among healthcare providers and patients alike.

Collaboration among various stakeholders is also vital in combating bias in AI. Healthcare professionals, data scientists, ethicists, and patient advocacy groups must work together to establish standards and guidelines for AI development. By fostering interdisciplinary partnerships, the healthcare industry can create more robust algorithms that account for the complexities of human health. Engaging patients in the conversation about AI can also provide valuable insights, ensuring that their needs and concerns are prioritized in the design of AI-driven solutions.

Finally, continuous education and training for healthcare professionals regarding AI technologies and their potential biases are essential. As the landscape of AI in healthcare evolves, it is critical for providers to stay informed about best practices for utilizing these tools effectively and ethically. By fostering a culture of awareness and responsibility, healthcare professionals can better navigate the challenges posed by bias in AI algorithms, ultimately leading to improved patient outcomes and a more equitable healthcare system.

The Future of AI Ethics in Healthcare

The future of AI ethics in healthcare is an essential consideration as technology continues to evolve and integrate into various aspects of medical practice. As artificial intelligence becomes increasingly prevalent in diagnostics, treatment planning, patient monitoring, and other healthcare functions, it raises important ethical questions about data privacy, informed consent, and the potential for bias. Stakeholders, including healthcare providers, patients, and policymakers, must work together to establish ethical frameworks that prioritize patient rights while fostering innovation in AI applications.

One of the primary ethical concerns in AI healthcare applications is the management of sensitive patient data. With AI-driven technologies collecting vast amounts of personal health information, ensuring that this data is protected from breaches and misuse is paramount. Establishing robust data governance policies can help safeguard patient privacy while allowing for the effective use of AI in improving healthcare outcomes. Transparency in how data is utilized, stored, and shared is crucial to maintaining trust between patients and healthcare providers.

Informed consent is another critical aspect of AI ethics in healthcare. Patients must be fully aware of how AI technologies will be used in their care, including the implications of algorithms in decision-making processes. Educating patients about AI's role in diagnostics, treatment recommendations, and monitoring can empower them to make informed choices about their healthcare. Clear communication about the benefits, risks, and limitations of AI tools is essential to fostering patient engagement and trust.

Bias in AI algorithms poses significant ethical challenges that need to be addressed. If the data used to train AI systems is not representative of diverse populations, the resulting algorithms may produce skewed outcomes that disproportionately affect certain groups. Ensuring equity in AI applications requires continuous evaluation of algorithms and the inclusion of diverse data sets. Healthcare organizations must actively work to identify and mitigate any biases in AI tools to promote fair and effective treatment for all patients.

As AI technologies advance, ethical considerations will continue to evolve. Ongoing dialogue among technologists, healthcare professionals, ethicists, and patients is necessary to adapt ethical frameworks to new developments in AI. By prioritizing ethical principles in the integration of AI into healthcare, stakeholders can harness its potential to enhance diagnostics, treatment planning, and patient engagement while safeguarding the values of equity, privacy, and patient autonomy. The future of AI ethics in healthcare will ultimately shape how these technologies improve health outcomes for individuals and communities alike.

Chapter 13: The Future of AI in Healthcare

Trends and Innovations on the Horizon

The integration of artificial intelligence in healthcare is poised to revolutionize how we approach diagnostics and treatment. A significant trend on the horizon is the advancement of AI-powered medical imaging analysis. This innovation enables more accurate and timely interpretations of imaging data, such as MRIs and CT scans. By employing advanced algorithms, AI can detect anomalies that may be missed by the human eye, leading to earlier diagnosis and intervention. As these technologies continue to evolve, we can expect a reduction in diagnostic errors and an overall improvement in patient outcomes.

Another promising development is the use of predictive analytics for disease outbreaks. By analyzing vast amounts of data from various sources, including social media, hospital records, and environmental factors, AI can identify patterns and predict potential outbreaks of infectious diseases. This proactive approach not only aids in timely public health responses but also equips healthcare providers with the insights needed to prepare and allocate resources effectively. As we harness these predictive capabilities, the healthcare system can shift from reactive to preventive strategies, ultimately safeguarding community health.

Personalized medicine is also experiencing a significant transformation driven by AI. Machine learning algorithms can analyze genetic information and other health data to tailor treatment plans to individual patients. This methodology allows for more effective interventions, as treatments can be customized based on a patient's unique genetic makeup and health history. The shift towards AI-driven personalized medicine emphasizes a more nuanced understanding of health, where treatments are no longer one-size-fits-all but instead are designed to maximize efficacy for each individual.

Real-time health data analytics stands out as a crucial innovation for patient monitoring. Utilizing wearable devices and mobile applications, AI can continuously collect and analyze data related to a patient's vital signs and lifestyle choices. This constant flow of information enables healthcare providers to monitor patients remotely, identify potential health issues early, and facilitate timely interventions. Such capabilities not only enhance patient engagement but also improve adherence to treatment plans, leading to better health outcomes and reduced hospital readmissions.

Lastly, the emergence of virtual health assistants and chatbots represents a new frontier in patient engagement and mental health support. These AI-driven tools offer immediate assistance for patients, providing information, answering questions, and even facilitating access to care. For individuals managing chronic conditions or seeking mental health support, these technologies create an accessible and responsive resource. As we continue to explore these innovations, the potential for AI to transform the healthcare landscape grows, promising a future where healthcare is more efficient, personalized, and responsive to the needs of all individuals.

The Integration of AI in Everyday Healthcare

The integration of artificial intelligence (AI) in everyday healthcare is transforming how individuals manage their health and interact with the medical system. AI technologies are increasingly being utilized to enhance diagnostics, treatment planning, and patient monitoring. This shift allows for more personalized and efficient healthcare solutions tailored to individual needs. By leveraging vast amounts of data, AI can assist healthcare professionals in making more informed decisions, ultimately leading to improved health outcomes for patients.

In diagnostics, AI systems analyze medical imaging and other diagnostic tests with remarkable accuracy. For example, AI-powered medical imaging analysis tools can detect early signs of diseases such as cancer, often more accurately than human radiologists. These tools not only increase the speed at which diagnoses can be made but also reduce the chances of human error. As a result, patients can receive timely interventions, which are crucial for conditions that require early treatment.Treatment planning has also seen significant advancements through AI integration. Predictive analytics can identify potential disease outbreaks and assess individual risk factors, allowing healthcare providers to develop tailored treatment plans based on a patient's unique genetic makeup and lifestyle. AI-driven personalized medicine enhances the effectiveness of treatments, as it considers the specific characteristics of a patient's condition, leading to better management of chronic diseases and improved outcomes in acute cases.

Patient monitoring has been revolutionized by AI technologies that provide real-time health data analytics. Wearable devices and mobile health applications can track vital signs, medication adherence, and other health metrics continuously. This data can be analyzed using AI algorithms to detect anomalies or trends that might indicate a worsening condition. Moreover, virtual health assistants engage patients in their care by providing reminders, answering medical queries, and facilitating access to health information, thereby empowering individuals to take control of their health.

Finally, the role of AI in supporting mental health through chatbots and automated workflow solutions for hospitals cannot be overstated. AI-driven chatbots offer immediate support and resources for individuals seeking help with mental health issues, making care more accessible. Simultaneously, automation in hospital settings streamlines operations, enabling healthcare providers to focus more on patient care rather than administrative tasks. As these technologies continue to evolve, the integration of AI in everyday healthcare will pave the way for a more responsive, efficient, and personalized healthcare system that benefits all individuals in their health journeys.

Preparing for an AI-Driven Future in Health

Preparing for an AI-Driven Future in Health involves understanding how artificial intelligence will reshape various aspects of healthcare. As individuals increasingly take an active role in managing their health, knowledge about AI applications becomes essential. AI technologies are poised to enhance diagnostics, treatment planning, patient monitoring, and overall healthcare delivery. This shift not only promises improved outcomes but also empowers patients to make informed decisions about their health.One significant area where AI is making strides is in diagnostics. Advanced algorithms analyze medical images with precision, identifying conditions that may be missed by the human eye. For example, AI-powered medical imaging analysis can detect early signs of diseases such as cancer, leading to timely interventions. As patients become familiar with these technologies, they can advocate for their use in their own diagnostic processes, ensuring they receive the most accurate assessments possible.

In treatment planning, AI-driven systems can analyze a wealth of data to recommend personalized treatment options tailored to individual needs. This personalized medicine approach considers genetic information, lifestyle factors, and existing health conditions, allowing for more effective and targeted therapies. Patients should stay informed about these advancements and engage in discussions with their healthcare providers about the potential benefits of AI-driven treatment plans tailored specifically for them.

Moreover, AI plays a pivotal role in patient monitoring and engagement. Virtual health assistants and chatbots facilitate continuous communication between healthcare providers and patients, offering support and information whenever needed. These tools can help manage chronic conditions by reminding patients to take medications or follow treatment protocols. By utilizing these technologies, patients can actively participate in their health management, leading to better adherence and improved outcomes.

Preparing for an AI-driven future also means understanding the broader implications of predictive analytics for disease outbreaks and AI in drug discovery. By analyzing patterns in health data, AI can predict potential outbreaks, enabling proactive measures to protect communities. Additionally, AI enhances the drug development process, making it faster and more efficient. As these technologies evolve, patients must remain engaged and informed, ensuring they can leverage AI-driven advancements for better health outcomes.

Chapter 14: Conclusion

The Journey of AI in Healthcare

The journey of artificial intelligence in healthcare has been marked by remarkable advancements and transformative potential. Initially, AI's role was largely limited to data analysis, where it assisted researchers in sifting through vast amounts of medical literature and patient records. Over the years, however, the technology has evolved significantly, moving beyond simple analytical tasks to more complex applications in diagnostics and treatment. This evolution has been driven by the increasing availability of large datasets, the development of sophisticated algorithms, and a growing recognition of AI's ability to enhance clinical decision-making and improve patient outcomes.

In the realm of diagnostics, AI technologies have revolutionized how conditions are identified and managed. Machine learning algorithms are now capable of analyzing medical images with unprecedented accuracy, often outperforming human radiologists in detecting conditions such as tumors and fractures. These advancements are not only speeding up the diagnostic process but also reducing the likelihood of human error. Furthermore, AI is being utilized in predictive analytics to foresee disease outbreaks, allowing healthcare systems to implement timely interventions. This proactive approach is essential in managing public health and mitigating the effects of infectious diseases.

Treatment planning has also seen significant enhancements through AI integration. With the ability to analyze patient data and treatment histories, AI systems can recommend personalized treatment plans that align with individual needs and preferences. This personalized medicine approach considers genetic factors, lifestyle choices, and environmental influences, enabling healthcare providers to offer tailored therapies that enhance efficacy and reduce side effects. Additionally, AI-driven virtual health assistants are emerging as crucial tools for patient engagement, guiding patients through treatment protocols and providing real-time support, which fosters adherence and better health management.Patient monitoring has been transformed through the use of AI-powered devices and applications that continuously collect and analyze health data. Wearable technologies and smart sensors provide healthcare professionals with real-time insights into patients' conditions, allowing for timely interventions and adjustments to treatment plans. This level of monitoring is particularly beneficial for chronic disease management, where consistent oversight is essential for preventing complications. AI's role in rehabilitation programs is also noteworthy, as it tailors recovery strategies based on individual progress, enhancing rehabilitation outcomes and patient satisfaction.

As AI continues to evolve, its applications in drug discovery and development are becoming increasingly prominent. AI algorithms can analyze biological data to identify potential drug candidates much faster than traditional methods, significantly reducing research and development timelines. Moreover, automated workflow solutions in hospitals are streamlining administrative tasks, allowing healthcare professionals to focus more on patient care. Chatbots are emerging as valuable tools for mental health support, providing immediate assistance and resources to those in need. The journey of AI in healthcare is just beginning, and its potential to reshape the landscape of health management is immense, promising a future where diagnostics, treatment, and patient engagement are all enhanced through intelligent technology.

Embracing Change for Better Health Outcomes

Embracing change is essential for improving health outcomes, particularly as advancements in artificial intelligence (AI) continue to reshape the landscape of healthcare. With the integration of AI technologies, individuals are presented with unprecedented opportunities to enhance their health management strategies. This shift not only facilitates better diagnostics and treatment plans but also empowers patients to take a more active role in their health journeys. As we explore the various dimensions of AI in healthcare, it is crucial to understand how these innovations can lead to significant improvements in health outcomes.

AI in diagnostics plays a pivotal role in early detection and accurate identification of diseases. By utilizing machine learning algorithms, healthcare providers can analyze vast amounts of data to identify patterns and anomalies that may indicate health issues. This capability not only enhances the accuracy of diagnostic procedures but also reduces the time it takes to reach a diagnosis. For individuals managing their health, this means potentially catching diseases at an earlier stage, leading to better treatment options and outcomes. As people become more aware of these technologies, they can advocate for their use in routine health assessments.

In the realm of treatment planning, AI offers tailored approaches that can significantly improve patient outcomes. By analyzing individual health data, AI-driven systems can recommend personalized treatment plans that consider a person's unique medical history, genetic predispositions, and lifestyle factors. This level of customization enhances the efficacy of treatments while minimizing adverse effects. As patients become more informed about their treatment options through AI, they can engage in meaningful conversations with their healthcare providers, ensuring that their preferences and needs are prioritized.

Patient monitoring has also evolved significantly with the advent of AI technologies. Wearable devices equipped with AI can track vital signs and other health metrics in real time, providing individuals with immediate feedback on their health status. This continuous monitoring allows for timely interventions, whether it be adjusting medications or seeking medical attention before a condition escalates. Embracing these tools not only increases awareness of one's health but also fosters a proactive approach to managing chronic conditions or preventing potential health crises.

Lastly, the integration of AI-powered virtual health assistants and chatbots has transformed patient engagement and support. These tools provide round-the-clock access to health information, guidance on managing symptoms, and even mental health support. For individuals taking charge of their health, these resources can enhance their understanding of their conditions and empower them to make informed decisions. By embracing these changes and leveraging AI technologies, patients can significantly improve their health outcomes and overall quality of life. The future of health is indeed bright, with AI leading the way toward a more personalized, efficient, and effective healthcare system.

Call to Action for Healthcare Stakeholders

Healthcare stakeholders must recognize the transformative potential of artificial intelligence in improving health outcomes for individuals. The integration of AI into various facets of healthcare—ranging from diagnostics to treatment planning—offers unprecedented opportunities for enhancing patient care. As individuals increasingly seek to take charge of their health, it is essential for healthcare providers, technology developers, and policymakers to collaborate and create an environment that supports the responsible deployment of AI technologies. This collaboration will ultimately empower patients to make informed decisions about their health and well-being.

In diagnostics, AI systems can analyze vast datasets to identify patterns that may elude even the most experienced healthcare professionals. Stakeholders should advocate for the adoption of AI-driven diagnostic tools that not only enhance accuracy but also reduce the time required to reach a diagnosis. By leveraging machine learning algorithms, healthcare providers can deliver personalized assessments that consider individual patient histories and genetic factors. The goal is to ensure that every patient receives timely and precise diagnostics, which is critical for effective treatment planning.

Moreover, AI's role in treatment planning is equally vital. Stakeholders should prioritize the development of AI-powered solutions that facilitate personalized treatment strategies. These tools can analyze data from a multitude of sources, including clinical studies and real-time patient information, to recommend optimal treatment pathways tailored to each individual's unique circumstances. By embracing AI in treatment planning, healthcare providers can improve the effectiveness of therapies and enhance patient outcomes, ultimately leading to more successful management of chronic conditions and complex diseases.

Patient monitoring is another area where AI can significantly impact healthcare delivery. Real-time health data analytics and AI-driven virtual health assistants can help patients manage their conditions more effectively. Stakeholders must invest in these technologies to ensure that patients have access to ongoing support and guidance. This not only enhances patient engagement but also fosters a sense of accountability in managing one's health. Furthermore, AI-powered medical imaging analysis can aid in early detection of health issues, leading to timely interventions that can save lives.

Finally, as the healthcare landscape continues to evolve, stakeholders must remain vigilant about the ethical implications of AI integration. It is crucial to establish frameworks that prioritize patient privacy and data security while promoting transparency in AI algorithms. By encouraging responsible AI development and usage, stakeholders can build trust among patients and healthcare providers alike. The future of health hinges on collective efforts to harness the power of AI, ensuring that it serves as a beneficial tool in the quest for better diagnostics and treatment.

Part-B(AI Revolution)

Chapter 1: Understanding AI

What is Artificial Intelligence?

Artificial Intelligence, commonly referred to as AI, encompasses a range of technologies that enable machines to perform tasks that typically require human intelligence. These tasks include understanding natural language, recognizing patterns, solving problems, and making decisions. At its core, AI can be categorized into two types: narrow AI and general AI. Narrow AI is designed to handle specific tasks, such as virtual assistants like Siri or Alexa, while general AI aims to perform any intellectual task that a human can do, although this remains largely theoretical at this point.

The development of AI is driven by advancements in computer science, data processing, and machine learning. Machine learning, a subset of AI, involves training algorithms on large datasets, allowing computers to learn from experience and improve their performance over time. Deep learning, a further specialization within machine learning, uses neural networks to analyze vast amounts of data, enabling machines to recognize complex patterns. This technological evolution has led to AI applications across various sectors, including healthcare, finance, transportation, and entertainment.

AI is increasingly becoming a part of our everyday lives, often in ways that go unnoticed. From recommendation algorithms on streaming platforms to customer service chatbots, AI technologies are enhancing user experiences and making processes more efficient. Smart home devices, powered by AI, learn user preferences and can automate tasks such as adjusting lighting, temperature, and security systems. As these technologies continue to evolve, AI is poised to play an even more significant role in shaping our daily routines and interactions.

Emerging trends in AI indicate a rapid expansion of its capabilities and applications. Developments in natural language processing are making it easier for machines to understand and generate human language, leading to more intuitive interfaces. Robotics is also advancing, with AI-driven robots being deployed in various fields, from manufacturing to healthcare, improving productivity and safety. Additionally, the integration of AI with other technologies, such as the Internet of Things (IoT), is creating a more interconnected and intelligent ecosystem, where devices can communicate and collaborate seamlessly.

Preparing for an AI-driven future requires a proactive approach to understanding and adapting to these changes. As AI continues to permeate different aspects of life, individuals and communities must embrace lifelong learning to stay informed about technological advancements. This includes developing digital literacy skills and being aware of the ethical implications of AI, such as privacy concerns and bias in algorithms. By fostering a culture of adaptability and curiosity, we can navigate the challenges and opportunities presented by AI, ensuring that its benefits are accessible to all.

A Brief History of AI

The history of artificial intelligence (AI) spans several decades, marked by significant milestones that have shaped its evolution. The concept of AI can be traced back to the mid-20th century when pioneers like Alan Turing and John McCarthy began exploring the idea of machines that could simulate human intelligence. Turing's famous 1950 paper, "Computing Machinery and Intelligence," proposed the Turing Test, a criterion for determining whether a machine could exhibit intelligent behavior indistinguishable from that of a human. This foundational work laid the groundwork for future developments in the field.

In the 1950s and 1960s, AI research gained momentum, particularly with the advent of early computer programs that could perform tasks deemed intelligent, such as playing chess and solving mathematical problems. Notably, the Logic Theorist, developed by Allen Newell and Herbert A. Simon, became one of the first programs to demonstrate reasoning abilities. During this period, the excitement surrounding AI led to ambitious predictions about the imminent arrival of fully intelligent machines, creating a sense of optimism that would later be met with challenges.

The subsequent decades brought about what is often referred to as the "AI winter," a period marked by diminished funding and interest due to the limitations of existing technologies. Researchers faced significant hurdles in achieving the grand visions of AI, leading to skepticism about its feasibility. However, the 1980s saw a resurgence of interest, driven by advancements in machine learning, expert systems, and the development of more powerful computers. This revival laid the foundation for the AI applications we see today, as researchers began to harness the capabilities of these emerging technologies.

The turn of the century marked a pivotal shift in AI development, fueled by the exponential growth of data and improvements in computational power. The rise of the internet created vast amounts of information that AI systems could analyze and learn from. Breakthroughs in deep learning, particularly through neural networks, allowed machines to process and understand data in ways that were previously unimaginable. This era witnessed remarkable achievements, such as IBM's Watson winning on the quiz show "Jeopardy!" and Google's

AlphaGo defeating a world champion Go player, showcasing AI's potential to outperform humans in complex tasks.

Today, AI has permeated various aspects of everyday life, from virtual assistants like Siri and Alexa to personalized recommendations on streaming platforms and e-commerce sites. As we look to the future, emerging trends in AI will continue to transform industries, enhancing productivity and creating new opportunities. Understanding the historical context of AI helps us navigate this rapidly evolving landscape, preparing us for an AI-driven future where these technologies will increasingly influence our daily experiences and societal structures.

Types of AI: Narrow vs. General

Artificial Intelligence (AI) can be broadly categorized into two main types: Narrow AI and General AI. Narrow AI, also known as Weak AI, refers to systems designed to perform specific tasks or solve particular problems. These AI systems excel in their designated areas, such as facial recognition, language translation, or playing strategic games like chess. Most of the AI applications we encounter today fall under this category. For instance, virtual assistants like Siri and Alexa utilize narrow AI to respond to user queries and perform tasks based on set commands, showcasing the technology's ability to enhance our daily lives.

In contrast, General AI, or Strong AI, represents a theoretical form of artificial intelligence that possesses the ability to understand, learn, and apply knowledge across a broad range of tasks, similar to human intelligence. General AI would be capable of reasoning, problem-solving, and even creativity, making it adaptable to new situations without requiring specific programming for each task. While this concept captures the imagination of researchers and futurists alike, it remains largely speculative, with no existing systems demonstrating true general intelligence as of now.

One of the significant implications of the distinction between Narrow and General AI is how each type impacts various industries and sectors. Narrow AI has already transformed fields such as healthcare, finance, and transportation by automating processes, improving efficiency, and providing data-driven insights. For example, in healthcare, AI algorithms analyze medical images to assist in diagnosing diseases more accurately and quickly than human practitioners. As these technologies continue to evolve, they promise to enhance productivity and improve decision-making across multiple domains.

However, the potential for General AI raises questions about its implications for society and the workforce. If achieved, General AI could revolutionize industries by performing complex tasks that currently require human intellect. This could lead to significant shifts in job markets, necessitating a reevaluation of the skills required in the future workforce. As society braces for the possibility of General AI, it becomes crucial for individuals to adapt by acquiring skills that complement AI technologies, ensuring they remain relevant in an increasingly automated world.

As we navigate the current landscape dominated by Narrow AI, it is essential to remain informed about emerging trends and the future developments in AI technology. By understanding the differences between Narrow and General AI, individuals can better prepare for an AI-driven future. Embracing these changes and recognizing the benefits of AI in everyday life will empower people to leverage technology effectively, ensuring they are equipped to thrive in a world where artificial intelligence plays an integral role.

The Role of Machine Learning

The role of machine learning in the AI revolution is pivotal, as it serves as the backbone for many applications that impact everyday life. Machine learning, a subset of artificial intelligence, involves algorithms that allow computers to learn from and make predictions or decisions based on data. This capability enables machines to improve their performance over time without being explicitly programmed for specific tasks. As machine learning continues to evolve, its integration into various sectors is transforming how we interact with technology, making it increasingly accessible and beneficial for common people.

One of the most noticeable impacts of machine learning is in the realm of personal assistance. Virtual assistants like Siri, Alexa, and Google Assistant utilize machine learning algorithms to understand voice commands more effectively and provide relevant responses. These systems analyze vast amounts of data to recognize speech patterns and contextual cues, allowing them to offer more accurate assistance in tasks ranging from setting reminders to controlling smart home devices. As these technologies advance, they are becoming more intuitive, enhancing user experience and convenience in daily routines.

In addition to personal assistants, machine learning is revolutionizing industries such as healthcare, finance, and transportation. In healthcare, machine learning algorithms analyze patient data to identify patterns that can lead to early diagnosis and personalized treatment plans. In finance, they are used to detect fraudulent transactions and assess credit risk, ensuring safer and more efficient banking services. Similarly, in transportation, machine learning powers navigation systems and autonomous vehicles, optimizing routes and improving safety. These advancements illustrate how machine learning is not just a technological trend but a fundamental change in how industries operate.

Education is another area where machine learning is making significant strides, personalizing learning experiences for students. Adaptive learning platforms utilize machine learning to assess individual learning styles and progress, tailoring educational content accordingly. This individualized approach helps students grasp concepts at their own pace and promotes better retention of knowledge. As educational institutions increasingly adopt these technologies, the potential for improved learning outcomes becomes more apparent, preparing students for a future where digital literacy is essential.

As we look towards an AI-driven future, it is crucial for common people to understand the implications of machine learning in their lives. By being aware of how these technologies work and their potential benefits, individuals can better prepare for changes in the job market and the economy. Embracing lifelong learning and acquiring new skills will be essential, as many traditional jobs may evolve or disappear due to automation. By staying informed and adaptable, everyone can thrive in a world increasingly shaped by machine learning and artificial intelligence.

Chapter 2: The Future of AI

Predictions for AI Development

As we look ahead, predictions for AI development suggest a landscape that will significantly impact everyday life. Advancements in machine learning and natural language processing are expected to enhance the capabilities of AI systems, making them more intuitive and accessible. This evolution means that AI will increasingly become a part of our daily routines, from virtual assistants that understand context to smart home devices that anticipate our needs. The integration of AI into daily life will transform how we interact with technology, leading to greater efficiency and convenience.

Emerging trends indicate that AI will not only refine existing technologies but also give rise to new applications. Industries such as healthcare, transportation, and education are poised for remarkable changes. For instance, AI-driven diagnostics can analyze medical images and predict health issues more accurately than ever before. In education, personalized learning experiences powered by AI will cater to individual student needs, enhancing engagement and knowledge retention. These developments will likely lead to improved outcomes and a more personalized experience in various sectors, fundamentally altering our interactions with them.

The rise of AI will also bring about significant changes in the job market. Automation may replace certain roles, but it will simultaneously create new opportunities in fields that require human oversight, creativity, and emotional intelligence. As AI takes on repetitive tasks, workers will need to adapt by acquiring new skills relevant to an AI-driven economy. Lifelong learning will become essential, and educational institutions will need to focus on equipping individuals with the skills necessary to thrive alongside AI technologies.

Moreover, ethical considerations surrounding AI development will become increasingly important. As AI systems become more autonomous, questions about accountability, bias, and transparency will need to be addressed. Public discourse regarding the ethical use of AI will shape regulations and guidelines that govern its development and application. Engaging in these conversations will be crucial for ensuring that AI technology serves the greater good and reflects societal values.

In conclusion, the predictions for AI development point towards a future where AI is deeply integrated into our lives, enhancing convenience, efficiency, and personalization. As we navigate this transition, it will be vital for individuals to stay informed and proactive in adapting to the changing landscape. By embracing new technologies and engaging in discussions about ethical implications, we can collectively shape a future that maximizes the benefits of AI while minimizing its risks. The journey ahead holds promise, and with preparation, we can thrive in an AI-driven world.

The Impact of AI on Jobs and Employment

The advent of artificial intelligence (AI) is reshaping the job landscape in unprecedented ways. As AI technologies become increasingly integrated into various industries, they are transforming the nature of work and the skills required to perform jobs. This shift presents both challenges and opportunities for the workforce. Many traditional roles may face obsolescence, while new positions are emerging that require a different set of skills. Understanding the implications of AI on employment is essential for individuals to navigate this evolving landscape effectively.

One of the most significant impacts of AI is the automation of routine and repetitive tasks. Jobs that involve manual labor or basic data processing are particularly susceptible to displacement by AI systems capable of performing these functions more efficiently. For instance, roles in manufacturing, data entry, and even some customer service positions are increasingly being handled by machines and algorithms. This trend raises concerns about job security for many workers who may find their roles diminished or eliminated altogether, highlighting the need for a proactive approach to workforce development.

Conversely, the rise of AI is also creating new job opportunities that did not exist a decade ago. Fields such as AI development, machine learning, and data analysis are experiencing rapid growth, necessitating a workforce skilled in these areas. Additionally, jobs that require human qualities such as creativity, emotional intelligence, and complex problem-solving are becoming increasingly valuable. As automation takes over routine tasks, there is a greater demand for individuals who can manage and interpret AI systems, suggesting a shift towards roles that emphasize collaboration between humans and technology.

Preparing for an AI-driven future requires individuals to adapt their skills and knowledge. Lifelong learning will be crucial as workers seek to stay relevant in their fields. Upskilling and reskilling initiatives will become vital for those whose jobs are at risk of automation. Educational institutions and employers must prioritize training programs that equip individuals with the skills needed to thrive in an AI-enhanced job market. Embracing technology and developing competencies in areas such as coding, data analysis, and digital literacy can empower workers to seize new opportunities created by AI advancements.

In summary, the impact of AI on jobs and employment is multifaceted, presenting both challenges and opportunities. While certain roles may become obsolete due to automation, new job categories are emerging that require a different skill set. The key to thriving in this rapidly changing environment lies in adaptability and a commitment to continuous learning. By understanding these dynamics and proactively preparing for the future, individuals can position themselves to benefit from the AI revolution rather than be left behind.

AI in Healthcare: Innovations on the Horizon

AI is poised to revolutionize healthcare by introducing innovative solutions that enhance patient care, streamline operations, and improve overall health outcomes. One of the most promising developments on the horizon is the use of AI algorithms to analyze vast amounts of medical data. By processing patient records, lab results, and imaging studies, AI can identify patterns that may go unnoticed by human clinicians. This capability can lead to earlier diagnoses of diseases, personalized treatment plans, and ultimately, more effective patient management.

Another significant innovation is the integration of AI-powered predictive analytics in medical settings. These tools can forecast patient outcomes based on historical data, helping healthcare providers to make informed decisions. For instance, AI can predict which patients are at higher risk for complications following surgery or which individuals may benefit most from preventive care measures. This predictive ability not only enhances patient safety but also optimizes resource allocation within healthcare systems, reducing costs and improving efficiency.

Telemedicine, already gaining traction, is expected to evolve further with AI's involvement. Virtual consultations powered by AI can assist healthcare professionals by providing real-time data analysis during patient interactions. For example, AI can analyze a patient's speech patterns or facial expressions to detect signs of distress or cognitive decline, thereby enriching the information available to doctors. This integration of AI into telehealth services will facilitate more accurate assessments and personalized care, making healthcare more accessible to patients regardless of their location.

Additionally, AI is set to transform drug discovery and development processes. Traditional methods of pharmaceutical research can be time-consuming and costly, often taking years to bring a new drug to market. AI can accelerate this process by simulating how drugs interact with biological systems, identifying potential candidates faster, and predicting their efficacy and safety. This innovation not only shortens development timelines but also increases the likelihood of success, ultimately leading to more treatment options for patients.

As these innovations unfold, it is essential for individuals to prepare for an AI-driven healthcare future. Understanding how AI will impact personal health management, from wearable devices that monitor vital signs to apps that offer personalized health advice, will empower people to take proactive roles in their healthcare journeys. Embracing these advancements and advocating for ethical AI practices in healthcare will ensure that the benefits of this revolution are realized equitably, ultimately leading to a healthier society.

AI and Climate Change Solutions

AI has emerged as a powerful tool in the fight against climate change, offering innovative solutions to some of the most pressing environmental challenges of our time. By leveraging vast amounts of data and advanced algorithms, AI systems can analyze complex climate patterns, predict environmental changes, and recommend actionable strategies to mitigate the impacts of climate change. This technology enables researchers, policymakers, and businesses to make more informed decisions that can lead to sustainable practices and reduced carbon footprints.

One of the most promising applications of AI in addressing climate change is in the energy sector. AI algorithms can optimize energy consumption in real-time, allowing for more efficient use of resources. Smart grids powered by AI can balance supply and demand, integrating renewable energy sources such as solar and wind more effectively. This not only reduces reliance on fossil fuels but also helps to stabilize energy prices. Moreover, AI can assist in predicting energy production from renewable sources, enabling better planning and investment in green technologies.

In agriculture, AI is transforming how we grow and manage crops, leading to more sustainable practices. Precision agriculture uses AI-driven insights to optimize planting schedules, irrigation, and pest control, which can significantly decrease resource use and waste. By analyzing weather patterns and soil conditions, AI tools can provide farmers with tailored recommendations, enhancing yields while minimizing environmental impact. This shift towards smarter farming practices is crucial for ensuring food security in a changing climate while reducing the agricultural sector's greenhouse gas emissions.

Transportation is another critical area where AI can contribute to climate change solutions. AI technologies are being integrated into public transport systems, helping to reduce congestion and emissions. Self-driving cars and intelligent traffic management systems can optimize travel routes, reduce fuel consumption, and lower carbon emissions. Additionally, AI can facilitate the development of electric vehicles by improving battery technology and charging infrastructure, making sustainable transportation more accessible to the general public.

As individuals, we can also harness the power of AI in our daily lives to contribute to climate change solutions. From smart home devices that manage energy use to apps that track personal carbon footprints, AI can help us make more sustainable choices. By understanding our consumption patterns, we can identify areas for improvement and adopt greener habits. As AI continues to evolve, its integration into our daily routines will play a crucial role in fostering a more sustainable future, empowering everyone to take part in the fight against climate change.

Chapter 3: Emerging Trends in AI

Natural Language Processing Advances

Natural Language Processing (NLP) has made significant strides in recent years, transforming the way humans interact with machines. This technology, which enables computers to understand, interpret, and generate human language, has become an integral part of our daily lives. From virtual assistants like Siri and Alexa to chatbots on websites, NLP enhances communication between people and devices. These advancements are not only reshaping the tech landscape but are also making technology more accessible and user-friendly for the average person.

One of the most notable advancements in NLP is the development of deep learning algorithms. These algorithms allow machines to learn from vast amounts of text data, improving their ability to comprehend context, sentiment, and nuance in language. This progression has led to more sophisticated applications, such as language translation services that can provide real-time translations with remarkable accuracy. The ability to communicate across language barriers is a game changer for global connectivity, enabling people to collaborate and share information regardless of their native tongue.

Moreover, NLP has significantly improved customer service experiences. Businesses are increasingly adopting AI-driven chatbots that can handle customer inquiries efficiently and round the clock. These chatbots utilize NLP to understand customer questions and provide immediate, relevant responses. This not only enhances customer satisfaction but also allows companies to allocate resources more effectively. As these systems become more advanced, they will likely take on more complex tasks, further streamlining business operations and improving user experiences.

In addition to customer service, NLP is also making inroads in education. Personalized learning platforms are harnessing the power of NLP to analyze student interactions and provide tailored feedback. By understanding how students communicate and the challenges they face, these platforms can adapt content to better suit individual learning styles. This technology has the potential to democratize education by making high-quality learning resources accessible to a broader audience, helping students gain knowledge in an engaging and efficient manner.

As we look toward the future, the implications of NLP advancements are vast. The integration of NLP into various aspects of everyday life promises to enhance productivity, foster creativity, and improve communication. However, it is also crucial for society to engage in discussions about the ethical use of these technologies. Ensuring that NLP is developed and applied responsibly will be essential to maximizing its benefits while minimizing potential risks. As we prepare for an AI-driven future, understanding and embracing these advances in NLP will empower individuals to adapt and thrive in an increasingly interconnected world.

AI in Autonomous Vehicles

The development of artificial intelligence has significantly transformed the automotive industry, leading to the rise of autonomous vehicles. These vehicles, often referred to as self-driving cars, utilize complex algorithms, machine learning, and vast amounts of data to navigate roads without human intervention. The integration of AI into vehicles promises not only increased convenience for drivers but also aims to enhance road safety and reduce traffic congestion. As technology evolves, understanding the implications of AI in this domain becomes increasingly important for everyday consumers.

One of the most compelling benefits of AI in autonomous vehicles is the potential for improved safety. Human error is a leading cause of traffic accidents, and AI has the capability to minimize these errors through real-time data analysis and decision-making. Autonomous vehicles are equipped with advanced sensors and cameras that allow them to detect and respond to their environment with remarkable accuracy. By processing information faster than a human driver could, AI systems can react to potential hazards, adjust speed, and even predict the actions of other drivers or pedestrians, thereby significantly reducing the likelihood of accidents.

Beyond safety, AI in autonomous vehicles could revolutionize urban mobility. As cities become increasingly congested, self-driving technology offers a solution to streamline transportation. Autonomous vehicles can optimize routes, reducing travel time and fuel consumption. This efficiency not only benefits individual passengers but also has the potential to lessen the overall strain on public transportation systems and road infrastructure. As cities implement smart traffic management systems that integrate with autonomous vehicles, the dream of more organized and efficient urban environments becomes a tangible reality.

Moreover, the rise of AI in autonomous vehicles raises important questions about the future of work and employment. As self-driving technology becomes more prevalent, industries related to transportation—such as trucking, delivery services, and taxi services—may see significant shifts. While some jobs may be displaced, new opportunities will likely emerge in areas such as vehicle maintenance, AI system development, and data analysis. Preparing for these changes requires individuals to adapt and acquire new skills that align with the evolving job landscape, emphasizing the importance of education and training in an AI-driven economy.

As we embrace the future of AI in autonomous vehicles, it is essential for consumers to stay informed and engaged. Understanding the technology behind self-driving cars, their benefits, and the challenges they pose will empower individuals to make informed decisions about their transportation options. Additionally, public discussions around regulations, ethical considerations, and safety standards will be critical as society navigates this transformative period. By participating in these conversations, the common person can play an active role in shaping a future where AI enhances everyday life while ensuring safety and accessibility for all.

AI and the Internet of Things (IoT)

AI and the Internet of Things (IoT) are converging to reshape how we interact with the world around us. The IoT consists of interconnected devices that communicate and share data over the internet, ranging from smart home appliances to industrial machines. When artificial intelligence is integrated into these devices, it enhances their capabilities, enabling them to learn from data, make decisions, and optimize performance. This synergy not only improves efficiency but also transforms our daily experiences, making them more intuitive and responsive to our needs.

One of the most visible applications of AI in IoT is in smart homes. Devices like thermostats, lighting systems, and security cameras can now learn user preferences and behaviors. For instance, a smart thermostat can analyze your heating and cooling habits to adjust temperatures efficiently, reducing energy consumption and costs. Similarly, smart security systems can recognize familiar faces or detect unusual activity, sending alerts to homeowners in real-time. These advancements contribute to a more comfortable and secure living environment, showcasing how AI can enhance everyday life.

In industrial settings, AI-powered IoT devices are revolutionizing manufacturing and supply chain management. Sensors embedded in machinery can monitor performance and predict maintenance needs, minimizing downtime and increasing productivity. For example, a factory equipped with AI-enabled IoT can analyze data from various production lines to identify inefficiencies and suggest improvements. This proactive approach not only saves time and resources but also fosters a culture of continuous improvement, which is essential for competitiveness in today's fast-paced market.

Healthcare is another area where AI and IoT are making significant strides. Wearable health devices, such as fitness trackers and smartwatches, collect valuable data about users' health metrics. AI algorithms analyze this data to provide personalized insights, helping individuals manage their health proactively. Moreover, connected medical devices can monitor patients remotely, alerting healthcare providers to any concerning changes in real-time. This integration of AI with IoT in healthcare enhances patient outcomes and streamlines the delivery of medical services, demonstrating the transformative potential of these technologies.

As we move further into an AI-driven future, it is important for individuals to understand and embrace these changes. The integration of AI with IoT will likely lead to more personalized services and smarter living environments. However, it also raises questions about privacy, security, and the ethical use of data. Preparing for this future involves staying informed about emerging trends and actively engaging in discussions about the implications of AI and IoT in our lives. By doing so, we can harness the benefits of these technologies while advocating for responsible practices that protect our rights and well-being.

Ethical AI: Challenges and Solutions

Ethical AI represents one of the most pressing challenges in the development and deployment of artificial intelligence technologies. As AI systems become increasingly integrated into everyday life, concerns about their ethical implications grow. Issues such as privacy, bias, accountability, and transparency are central to discussions about the responsible use of AI. For instance, algorithms that govern social media feeds or credit scoring can inadvertently reinforce existing societal biases, leading to unfair treatment of certain groups. This creates a pressing need for frameworks that ensure AI systems operate fairly and transparently, safeguarding the rights of individuals.

Addressing the challenges of ethical AI requires collaboration among multiple stakeholders, including technologists, policymakers, and ethicists. Engaging in open dialogues can help identify the potential harms associated with AI technologies and the best practices for mitigating these risks. For example, companies developing AI products can work with ethicists to conduct impact assessments that evaluate how their technologies might affect different demographics. This collaborative approach not only helps in identifying ethical pitfalls but also fosters a culture of accountability in AI development.

One of the key solutions to the ethical challenges posed by AI is the establishment of robust regulatory frameworks. Governments and international organizations can play a crucial role in creating guidelines that promote ethical AI practices. Such regulations could mandate transparency in AI algorithms, ensuring that users understand how decisions affecting them are made. Moreover, regulatory bodies can set standards for data privacy and security, demanding that organizations prioritize the protection of personal information. By instituting clear rules, society can hold AI developers accountable for their creations, ultimately fostering trust in these technologies.

Another effective strategy is the implementation of diverse teams in AI development. By including individuals from various backgrounds, perspectives, and experiences, organizations can reduce the risk of bias in AI systems. Diverse teams are more likely to recognize potential ethical issues and consider the broader societal implications of their work. Training programs focused on ethics in technology can further equip these teams with the knowledge needed to navigate complex moral landscapes. Promoting diversity not only enhances the ethical considerations in AI development but also leads to more innovative solutions that better meet the needs of a diverse population.

As the world continues to embrace AI technologies, the need for ethical considerations becomes increasingly critical. Individuals can prepare for an AI-driven future by staying informed about these ethical challenges and advocating for responsible practices in AI development. Engaging in community discussions, supporting organizations that prioritize ethical AI, and demanding accountability from tech companies are all ways that common people can contribute to a more ethical AI landscape. By collectively addressing these challenges, society can harness the transformative potential of AI while ensuring that it serves the common good.

Chapter 4: AI in Everyday Life

AI in Personal Assistants: Your Smart Home

AI in personal assistants has transformed the concept of smart homes, making them more intuitive and responsive to our daily needs. Smart home technology, powered by artificial intelligence, enables devices to learn user preferences and habits, leading to a more personalized living environment. These systems can control various aspects of the home, from lighting and heating to security and entertainment, all while adapting to the lifestyles of the inhabitants. As a result, managing home tasks becomes more efficient and less time-consuming, allowing individuals to focus on what truly matters in their lives.

One of the most prominent features of AI in personal assistants is voice recognition. Smart speakers and virtual assistants like Amazon's Alexa, Google Assistant, and Apple's Siri allow users to interact with their devices using natural language. This technology has made it easier for people to control their smart home devices without needing to navigate complicated apps or interfaces. Users can simply issue voice commands to adjust the thermostat, dim the lights, or play music, creating a seamless and enjoyable experience. This ease of use encourages wider adoption of smart home technology among people of all ages.

Another significant advantage of AI in personal assistants is their ability to automate routine tasks. Smart home systems can schedule and execute various functions automatically, such as watering plants, adjusting the thermostat when no one is home, or locking doors at night. Such automation not only saves time but also enhances energy efficiency. For instance, smart thermostats learn when to lower or raise temperatures based on occupancy patterns, resulting in reduced energy consumption and lower utility bills. This kind of proactive management of home resources represents a significant step toward sustainable living.

Security is another critical area where AI enhances smart homes. Advanced AI algorithms analyze data from security cameras and sensors to identify unusual activities or potential threats. Users can receive real-time alerts on their smartphones, enabling them to monitor their homes remotely. Additionally, AI can distinguish between familiar faces and strangers, reducing false alarms and providing a sense of safety. This integration of AI into home security systems not only provides peace of mind but also empowers homeowners to take control of their security measures.

As AI continues to evolve, the future of personal assistants in smart homes looks promising. Emerging trends indicate that these systems will become even more intuitive, capable of predicting user needs and making proactive suggestions. For example, a smart assistant might suggest preparing a meal based on dietary preferences and previous cooking habits or remind users to purchase groceries when supplies run low. As we embrace this AI-driven future, it is essential for individuals to stay informed and adapt to these changes, ensuring they can fully leverage the benefits of intelligent personal assistants in their daily lives.

AI in Entertainment: Recommendations and Content Creation

AI has become a transformative force in the entertainment industry, significantly altering how content is created, distributed, and consumed. One of the most notable applications of AI is in recommendation systems. Streaming platforms like Netflix and Spotify utilize sophisticated algorithms to analyze user behavior, preferences, and viewing habits. These systems can predict what content users are likely to enjoy, thereby personalizing the experience. By leveraging vast amounts of data, AI helps users discover new music, movies, and shows they might not have found otherwise, enhancing their engagement and satisfaction.

Content creation is another area where AI is making waves. Tools powered by machine learning and natural language processing are assisting writers, filmmakers, and artists in generating new ideas and even entire pieces of content. For instance, AI algorithms can analyze existing narratives to identify popular themes and tropes, which can inspire writers in their work. Additionally, AI-generated scripts and storylines are being tested in various creative industries, showcasing the potential for AI to collaborate with human creators. This symbiosis not only speeds up the creative process but also opens up new avenues for innovative storytelling.

Moreover, AI plays a crucial role in enhancing visual effects and animation. In the film industry, AI technologies are employed to streamline the production process, allowing for more complex visual effects to be created with greater efficiency. For example, AI can automate tedious tasks such as rotoscoping, where animators outline frames to create realistic movements. This not only saves time but also allows artists to focus on more creative aspects of their projects. As a result, audiences are treated to visually stunning content that pushes the boundaries of traditional filmmaking.

The rise of AI in entertainment also raises questions about the nature of creativity and authorship. As AI becomes more involved in the creative process, concerns about originality and intellectual property come to the forefront. Who owns the rights to an AI-generated piece of art? Can a machine truly be considered a creator? These questions challenge our understanding of creativity and may lead to new legal and ethical frameworks in the arts. Engaging in this dialogue is essential as society navigates the implications of AI's growing influence in creative fields.

Looking to the future, the integration of AI in entertainment is likely to deepen, with emerging trends promising even more personalized and immersive experiences. Virtual reality and augmented reality technologies, enhanced by AI, could create fully interactive environments tailored to individual preferences. As audiences increasingly demand unique and engaging content, the entertainment industry will continue to experiment with AI applications, shaping the way we experience art, music, and storytelling in an increasingly digital world. Embracing these advancements and preparing for their impact will be crucial for consumers as they navigate the evolving landscape of entertainment.

AI in Education: Personalized Learning Experiences

AI is transforming education by enabling personalized learning experiences tailored to the needs of individual students. Traditional educational models often adopt a one-size-fits-all approach, which can leave many students disengaged or struggling to keep pace with their peers. With advancements in artificial intelligence, educators can now harness data and algorithms to create customized learning paths that address each student's unique strengths, weaknesses, and preferences. This shift not only enhances student engagement but also fosters a deeper understanding of the material being taught.

One of the key benefits of AI in education is its ability to analyze vast amounts of data in real-time. Learning management systems equipped with AI can track students' progress, identify areas where they may be struggling, and suggest targeted resources to help them improve. For instance, if a student consistently performs poorly in math, the system can recommend specific practice exercises or tutorials that focus on the problematic concepts. This level of individualized support helps students take ownership of their learning while allowing teachers to focus on providing guidance and support rather than merely delivering content.

Moreover, AI-driven educational tools can adapt to the learning pace of each student, allowing for a more flexible and responsive learning environment. Some platforms use machine learning algorithms to adjust the difficulty of exercises based on a student's performance, ensuring that they are neither bored with overly simple tasks nor overwhelmed by challenges that are too difficult. This adaptability is particularly beneficial for diverse classrooms where students have varying levels of readiness and learning styles. As a result, students can progress at their own pace, leading to improved retention and a more positive attitude towards learning.

Additionally, AI can facilitate collaboration and engagement among students through interactive learning experiences. Tools powered by AI can create virtual environments where learners can work together on projects, participate in discussions, and receive instant feedback. For example, AI can analyze group dynamics and suggest roles for each student, helping to optimize teamwork and ensuring that all voices are heard. This collaborative approach not only enriches the learning experience but also helps students develop essential skills such as communication, problem-solving, and critical thinking, which are vital for success in the modern world.

As we move towards an AI-driven future, the implications for education are profound. Educators, students, and parents must embrace these technological advancements to prepare for a more personalized and effective learning experience. By leveraging AI, we can create a system that not only accommodates individual learning needs but also cultivates a love for lifelong learning. As AI continues to evolve, its integration into education will play a crucial role in shaping the skills and competencies of future generations, equipping them for the challenges and opportunities of an increasingly complex world.

AI in Customer Service: Chatbots and Beyond

AI technology has increasingly permeated customer service, transforming the way businesses interact with their customers. The advent of chatbots has been a significant milestone in this evolution. These AI-driven programs are designed to simulate human conversation, enabling them to handle a variety of customer inquiries efficiently. From answering frequently asked questions to assisting with product purchases, chatbots provide instant support, often available 24/7. This capability not only enhances customer satisfaction by reducing wait times but also allows companies to allocate human resources to more complex tasks that require personal attention.

As technology advances, the functionality of chatbots continues to improve. Modern chatbots utilize natural language processing (NLP) and machine learning algorithms to understand context and sentiment, allowing them to provide more personalized responses. This shift from simple keyword recognition to sophisticated conversational abilities means that chatbots can now engage in more meaningful interactions, leading to a better customer experience. Companies that leverage these advanced chatbots often see increased engagement and loyalty from their customer base, as users appreciate the tailored assistance they receive.

Beyond chatbots, AI in customer service is also manifesting through predictive analytics. Businesses are now able to analyze customer data to anticipate needs and preferences before they are even expressed. By understanding buying patterns and previous interactions, companies can proactively reach out to customers with relevant offers or support. This predictive capability not only enhances the service experience but also drives sales, as customers are more likely to engage with brands that understand and cater to their needs.

Moreover, AI tools are being integrated into customer service platforms, enabling human agents to work more efficiently. For instance, AI can assist agents by providing real-time suggestions during customer interactions, drawing from vast databases of information to offer solutions quickly. This collaborative approach between AI and human agents ensures that inquiries are resolved faster while maintaining a high level of service quality. The blend of AI efficiency and human empathy creates a more robust customer service framework, paving the way for improved customer relationships.

As we move towards an AI-driven future, it is crucial for individuals to understand how these technologies will reshape their interactions with businesses. Embracing AI in customer service is not just about enhancing efficiency; it is about creating a more responsive and personalized experience for consumers. As chatbots and other AI applications continue to evolve, the potential for improved customer service will only grow, urging both businesses and customers to adapt to this new landscape. Preparing for these changes will empower individuals to navigate an increasingly AI-integrated world with confidence and ease.

Chapter 5: Preparing for an AI-Driven Future

Skills for the Future Workforce

The rapid advancement of artificial intelligence is reshaping the workforce landscape, leading to a pressing need for individuals to cultivate a new set of skills. As automation and AI technologies become integrated into various industries, the demand for human roles is evolving. Skills that were once considered essential may no longer hold the same value, while new competencies are emerging as crucial for success in an AI-driven world. Understanding these skills is vital for anyone looking to thrive in the future job market.

One of the most important skills for the future workforce is digital literacy. As AI systems become more prevalent, individuals must be adept at using technology and understanding how it impacts their work and daily lives. Digital literacy goes beyond basic computer skills; it encompasses the ability to analyze data, engage with software tools, and leverage online resources effectively. This proficiency enables individuals to work alongside AI systems, making informed decisions and enhancing productivity.

Critical thinking and problem-solving skills are also paramount in an AI-dominated environment. While AI can process vast amounts of data and offer insights, it lacks the human ability to think creatively and approach problems from multiple angles. Workers will need to develop the capacity to analyze information critically, identify challenges, and design innovative solutions that machines may not be able to formulate on their own. Emphasizing these skills will empower individuals to complement AI technologies rather than be replaced by them.

Another essential skill is emotional intelligence, which encompasses self-awareness, empathy, and interpersonal skills. As AI takes over routine tasks, the human touch becomes increasingly valuable in the workplace. Roles that require effective communication, collaboration, and relationship-building will thrive, as machines cannot replicate the complexity of human emotions and social interactions. Individuals who cultivate emotional intelligence will be better equipped to navigate team dynamics and foster a positive work environment.

Finally, adaptability and a willingness to learn continuously are crucial in an era of rapid change. The pace of technological advancements means that new tools and methodologies will emerge frequently, requiring individuals to stay updated and flexible. Embracing lifelong learning through formal education, online courses, and hands-on experiences will help workers remain relevant and competitive. By fostering a mindset geared toward growth and transformation, individuals can effectively respond to the evolving demands of the workforce shaped by AI.

Understanding AI's Limitations

Understanding AI's limitations is crucial for anyone looking to navigate the rapidly evolving landscape of technology. While artificial intelligence has made remarkable strides, it is essential to recognize that it is not infallible. AI systems operate based on algorithms and data, which means they can only perform tasks within the parameters set by those inputs. This reliance on data can lead to biases, inaccuracies, and a lack of understanding in complex or nuanced situations. Acknowledging these limitations helps people set realistic expectations about what AI can and cannot do in their daily lives.

One significant limitation of AI is its inability to comprehend context in the way humans do. While AI can analyze vast amounts of data and identify patterns, it lacks the depth of understanding that comes from human experience. For example, an AI may excel at processing language, but it may struggle with sarcasm, humor, or emotional nuance. This can lead to misunderstandings or misinterpretations in applications such as customer service or social media interactions. Recognizing that AI lacks this contextual awareness is vital for users who rely on these technologies for communication or decision-making.

Another critical limitation is the dependence on data quality and quantity. AI systems learn from the data they are trained on, meaning that if the data is flawed or incomplete, the AI's output will also reflect those shortcomings. This can result in biased outcomes, particularly in areas like hiring processes or law enforcement. It is essential for individuals and organizations to be aware of the data sources feeding AI systems and to advocate for transparency and accountability in how these systems are developed and deployed. Understanding this aspect can empower users to question and challenge AI decisions that may adversely affect them.

Moreover, AI lacks creativity and emotional intelligence, which are vital in many aspects of life. While AI can generate content or mimic artistic styles, it cannot originate ideas or convey genuine emotion. This limitation becomes particularly evident in creative industries, such as writing, art, or music, where human intuition and inspiration play a crucial role. As AI tools become more prevalent in these fields, it's important for people to appreciate the unique qualities of human creativity that machines cannot replicate. This understanding can help maintain the value of human contributions while leveraging AI as a supportive tool rather than a replacement.

Lastly, the ethical implications of AI's limitations cannot be overlooked. As artificial intelligence systems are integrated into various sectors, including healthcare, finance, and education, the consequences of their limitations can have significant societal impacts. Issues such as data privacy, job displacement, and algorithmic bias highlight the need for a thoughtful approach to AI implementation. By understanding these limitations, individuals can engage in informed discussions about the ethical use of AI and advocate for practices that prioritize fairness, accountability, and human oversight. This proactive stance is essential for preparing for an AI-driven future that benefits everyone.

Embracing Lifelong Learning

Embracing lifelong learning is essential in the age of artificial intelligence, where rapid advancements are reshaping our world. As AI technologies continue to evolve, individuals must adapt by continually updating their knowledge and skills. The integration of AI into various aspects of daily life—from smart home devices to personalized recommendations—highlights the need for a proactive approach to learning. Understanding how these systems work and their implications can empower individuals to make informed decisions and leverage AI to enhance their lives.

One of the most significant trends in AI is its influence on the job market. Many traditional roles are being transformed or replaced by automation, leading to a growing demand for new skills. Embracing lifelong learning can help individuals stay relevant in their careers and explore new opportunities. Online courses, workshops, and community programs provide accessible avenues for skill development, enabling people to learn at their own pace and according to their interests. By actively seeking out educational resources, individuals can navigate the changing landscape of work with confidence.

In addition to career-related skills, lifelong learning encompasses understanding the ethical implications of AI. As AI systems become more integrated into society, issues such as privacy, bias, and accountability emerge. Educating oneself about these concerns is crucial for participating in discussions about AI policies and practices. Engaging with local forums, online communities, or reading relevant literature can deepen one's understanding of these ethical dimensions, empowering individuals to advocate for responsible AI use and contribute to shaping a future that aligns with societal values.

Moreover, embracing lifelong learning fosters adaptability, a vital trait in an ever-changing technological environment. As new AI tools and applications are developed, being open to learning allows individuals to experiment with and integrate these innovations into their lives. Whether it involves using AI-driven personal assistants, exploring data analysis tools, or understanding machine learning basics, a commitment to lifelong learning encourages curiosity and experimentation. This mindset not only enhances personal growth but also prepares individuals to embrace changes with resilience and creativity.

Ultimately, embracing lifelong learning is about cultivating a mindset that values growth and adaptability. In a world increasingly influenced by AI, the ability to learn continuously will determine how effectively individuals can navigate their personal and professional lives. By prioritizing education, staying informed about emerging trends, and actively engaging with new technologies, people can not only survive but thrive in an AI-driven future. This proactive approach to learning equips individuals with the tools they need to harness the benefits of AI while contributing positively to their communities and society at large.

Building Resilience in an AI World

Building resilience in an AI world is essential for navigating the rapid changes brought about by technological advancements. As artificial intelligence continues to evolve, it is reshaping the landscape of work, communication, and everyday life. Individuals must adapt to these changes, developing a mindset that embraces flexibility and learning. Resilience is not merely the ability to bounce back from challenges; it involves proactively equipping oneself with the skills and knowledge necessary to thrive in an AI-driven environment.

To build resilience, the first step is staying informed about emerging trends in AI. Understanding the technology behind AI, including its capabilities and limitations, enables individuals to make educated decisions in both personal and professional contexts. This knowledge can demystify AI, reducing fear and uncertainty. Engaging with educational resources, attending workshops, and participating in community discussions can foster a deeper comprehension of AI and its implications for various industries. By becoming well-versed in AI developments, individuals can anticipate changes and adapt more effectively.

Moreover, cultivating a growth mindset is vital in an AI world. As automation and machine learning increasingly take over routine tasks, individuals must focus on developing uniquely human skills such as creativity, emotional intelligence, and critical thinking. These attributes cannot easily be replicated by AI and will remain valuable in the workforce. Embracing lifelong learning, whether through formal education or self-directed study, can help individuals stay relevant and versatile. This adaptability not only enhances personal resilience but also contributes to overall career longevity in an evolving job market.

Community support plays a crucial role in fostering resilience amid the uncertainties of an AI-driven future. Building networks with like-minded individuals can provide encouragement and shared resources, creating a safety net during times of transition. Engaging in local initiatives focused on technology and AI can promote collaboration and idea-sharing, allowing individuals to learn from one another's experiences. Additionally, participating in discussions about ethical AI use and societal impacts can empower individuals to advocate for responsible practices, reinforcing their sense of agency in an AI world.

Finally, it is essential to maintain a balance between technology and personal well-being. As AI becomes more integrated into everyday life, individuals must be mindful of its impact on mental health and social interactions. Setting boundaries around technology use, prioritizing face-to-face communication, and engaging in hobbies outside of the digital realm can enhance resilience. By fostering emotional and psychological well-being, individuals can better navigate the complexities of an AI-driven world, ensuring that technology serves as a tool for empowerment rather than a source of stress.

Chapter 6: Navigating the Ethical Landscape of AI

Privacy Concerns in the Age of AI

As artificial intelligence becomes increasingly integrated into our daily lives, privacy concerns have emerged as a significant issue for consumers. With the proliferation of smart devices, social media platforms, and AI-driven applications, vast amounts of personal data are collected, processed, and stored. This data can include everything from browsing habits and purchasing preferences to location information and personal communications. While this information can enhance user experience by providing personalized services, it also raises important questions regarding who has access to this data, how it is used, and what measures are in place to protect it.

One of the primary concerns regarding privacy in the age of AI is the potential for misuse of personal information. Companies often collect data to improve their products and services, but this data can also be exploited for targeted advertising or, worse, sold to third parties without the users' consent. The lack of transparency in how data is handled can lead to a feeling of vulnerability among consumers, who may not fully understand what they are agreeing to when they accept terms and conditions. This highlights the need for clearer regulations and policies that protect individual privacy while still allowing for innovation in AI technology.

The rise of surveillance technologies powered by AI further complicates privacy issues. Governments and businesses have increasingly adopted AI tools for monitoring behavior, tracking movements, and analyzing communications. While proponents argue that these technologies can enhance security and efficiency, critics warn that they can infringe on civil liberties and create an environment of constant oversight. This balance between security and privacy is delicate and requires ongoing dialogue among stakeholders, including policymakers, technologists, and the public, to ensure that individual rights are not sacrificed in the name of progress.

Another factor contributing to privacy concerns is the potential for algorithmic bias, which can indirectly affect personal privacy. AI systems often learn from historical data, which may contain biases reflecting societal inequalities. If these biases are not addressed, they can lead to unfair treatment in areas such as employment, lending, and law enforcement. This raises ethical questions about accountability and the responsibility of AI developers to create systems that not only respect privacy but also promote fairness and equity in their applications.

As we move further into an AI-driven future, it is crucial for individuals to be proactive about their privacy. This includes being informed about the types of data being collected, the purposes for which it is used, and the rights they hold regarding their information. Consumers should take advantage of privacy settings, demand transparency from companies, and advocate for stronger regulations. By actively engaging with these issues, people can better protect their personal information and contribute to the development of a more ethical and responsible AI landscape.

Bias in AI: Understanding the Risks

Bias in AI can significantly affect how these technologies operate and the decisions they make. This bias often stems from the data used to train AI systems, which may reflect societal prejudices or imbalances. For instance, if an AI is trained on data that predominantly features one demographic, it may struggle to accurately represent or serve other groups. This can lead to discriminatory practices, where certain individuals or communities receive less favorable outcomes based solely on their identity. Understanding this risk is crucial as AI becomes increasingly integrated into various aspects of daily life.

The implications of biased AI are far-reaching. In sectors such as hiring, lending, and law enforcement, biased algorithms can perpetuate existing inequalities. An AI system used for recruitment might favor candidates from a specific background if its training data is skewed toward that demographic. Similarly, predictive policing algorithms could reinforce racial profiling by relying on historical crime data that reflects biased policing practices. These scenarios highlight the urgent need for transparency and accountability in AI development to ensure that these technologies do not inadvertently harm marginalized groups.

Mitigating bias in AI requires a multifaceted approach. Developers must prioritize diverse and representative datasets during the training phase. This involves actively seeking out and including data from underrepresented groups to create a more balanced perspective. Additionally, implementing rigorous testing and validation processes can help identify potential biases before the AI systems are deployed. Stakeholder collaboration, including input from ethicists, community representatives, and affected individuals, can further enhance the fairness and reliability of AI technologies.

Education plays a vital role in addressing bias in AI. As AI technologies become more prevalent, it is essential for the general public to understand how these systems work and the potential biases they may carry. By fostering an informed community, individuals can advocate for ethical AI practices and hold companies accountable for their products. Public discourse around AI should include discussions about the importance of fairness, transparency, and inclusivity to ensure that the benefits of AI advancements are shared equitably.

As we prepare for an AI-driven future, being aware of bias in AI is paramount. Individuals must engage with these technologies critically and demand responsible practices from developers and organizations. By collectively addressing the risks associated with biased AI, society can work towards a future where AI serves as a tool for empowerment rather than a source of division. Understanding and mitigating bias is not just a technical challenge; it is a moral imperative that shapes the societal landscape of tomorrow.

The Role of Regulation and Governance

Regulation and governance play a critical role in shaping the landscape of artificial intelligence, influencing how it develops and integrates into society. As AI technology continues to evolve at an unprecedented pace, the need for effective frameworks to manage its impact becomes increasingly essential. Regulations can help ensure that AI systems are developed and deployed responsibly, addressing ethical concerns, privacy issues, and potential biases. By establishing clear guidelines, governments and organizations can foster trust among users, encouraging wider adoption and acceptance of AI technologies in everyday life.

One of the primary objectives of regulation in the AI sector is to safeguard public interests. This involves creating standards that govern data privacy, security, and accountability. For instance, regulatory bodies can mandate transparency in AI algorithms, ensuring that users understand how decisions are made. This transparency is vital in preventing discrimination and bias, particularly when AI is applied in sensitive areas such as hiring, lending, and law enforcement. By holding companies accountable for their AI systems, regulations can help mitigate risks and protect vulnerable populations from harm.

Governance structures also play a pivotal role in promoting innovation while ensuring safety. A balanced approach to regulation allows for flexibility, enabling businesses and researchers to explore new AI applications without being stifled by overly restrictive rules. Collaborative governance models, which involve stakeholders from various sectors, can facilitate the sharing of knowledge and best practices. This collaborative spirit can lead to the development of innovative solutions that address societal challenges, from healthcare to climate change, while still adhering to ethical standards.

Moreover, international cooperation is essential in the realm of AI regulation. As AI technology knows no borders, harmonizing regulatory approaches across countries can help prevent regulatory arbitrage, where companies exploit lax regulations in certain jurisdictions. Global frameworks can enhance cooperation in research, development, and the sharing of data, ultimately leading to more robust AI systems. By aligning regulatory efforts internationally, countries can collectively address the challenges posed by AI, ensuring that advancements benefit humanity as a whole.

Finally, public engagement in the regulatory process is crucial to ensuring that the voice of the common people is heard. As AI becomes an integral part of daily life, individuals should have a say in how it is governed. This can be achieved through public consultations, educational initiatives, and inclusive policy-making processes. By empowering citizens to participate in discussions about AI regulation, societies can foster a sense of ownership and responsibility towards these technologies. In turn, this engagement can lead to more informed and equitable policies that reflect the needs and values of diverse communities.

Promoting Transparency in AI Systems

Promoting transparency in AI systems is crucial as artificial intelligence becomes more integrated into our daily lives. Transparency refers to the clarity and openness with which AI systems operate, enabling users to understand how decisions are made. As AI technologies evolve, they often become more complex, leading to a phenomenon known as the "black box" issue, where even the developers may not fully grasp how their algorithms reach specific conclusions. This lack of understanding can erode trust among users, making it essential to promote transparency in AI.

One of the primary ways to enhance transparency is through the development of explainable AI (XAI). Explainable AI aims to provide clear insights into the decision-making processes of AI systems. By leveraging techniques that allow users to interpret and understand AI outcomes, XAI can help demystify how algorithms function. For instance, if a healthcare AI suggests a particular treatment plan, it should ideally provide a rationale based on patient data, medical history, and relevant research. This empowers users to make informed decisions about their health, fostering trust in the technology.

Another important aspect of promoting transparency involves the ethical use of data. AI systems rely on vast amounts of data to learn and make decisions. Ensuring that this data is collected, stored, and used responsibly is vital for maintaining transparency. Users should be informed about what data is being collected, how it is used, and who has access to it. Implementing clear data governance policies can not only protect user privacy but also reassure individuals that their information is handled ethically, enhancing public confidence in AI systems.

Engagement with diverse stakeholders is also essential in promoting transparency. Developers, policymakers, and users must collaborate to create standards and guidelines that govern the use of AI. This multi-stakeholder approach can lead to the establishment of best practices for transparency, ensuring that a wide range of perspectives is considered. By involving the community in discussions about AI systems, developers can better address concerns and expectations, resulting in more user-centric solutions that prioritize transparency.

Finally, education plays a significant role in fostering transparency in AI systems. As AI continues to permeate various aspects of life, it is essential to equip individuals with the knowledge necessary to understand these technologies. Public awareness campaigns, workshops, and accessible online resources can empower users to engage with AI more critically. By demystifying AI and its processes, society can promote a culture of transparency, where individuals feel informed and confident in their interactions with AI systems, ultimately paving the way for a more equitable and trustworthy AI-driven future.

Chapter 7: Taking Action: How to Engage with AI

Staying Informed: Resources and Communities

In the rapidly evolving landscape of artificial intelligence, staying informed is essential for individuals who want to understand how these technologies impact their lives. The first step in this journey is identifying reliable resources that break down complex concepts into digestible information. Online platforms such as Coursera, edX, and Khan Academy offer courses that cater to various skill levels, from beginners to advanced learners. These platforms often collaborate with universities and industry experts to create content that is both informative and accessible. Additionally, websites like AI Weekly or MIT Technology Review provide curated news articles and analyses that keep readers up to date with the latest developments in AI.

Engaging with communities dedicated to AI can significantly enhance one's understanding and provide networking opportunities. Online forums like Reddit's r/MachineLearning or AI-focused Discord channels foster discussions among enthusiasts, professionals, and newcomers alike. Participating in these communities allows individuals to ask questions, share experiences, and gain insights from varied perspectives. Attending local meetups or conferences can also facilitate deeper connections and provide firsthand exposure to cutting-edge research and applications in AI. These interactions can bolster one's knowledge base and inspire personal or professional projects.

Social media platforms can also serve as valuable resources for staying informed about AI trends. Following thought leaders, researchers, and organizations in the AI space on Twitter or LinkedIn can provide a steady stream of updates, articles, and opinions. Many of these influencers share their insights on emerging technologies and ethical considerations surrounding AI, which can help individuals understand the broader implications of developments in this field. Additionally, social media can amplify voices from diverse backgrounds, allowing for a more comprehensive understanding of how AI affects various communities.

Podcasts and YouTube channels dedicated to AI offer another engaging way to absorb information. Programs like "The AI Alignment Podcast" or channels such as "Two Minute Papers" break down complex topics into entertaining formats. These resources often feature interviews with experts who discuss their work and the future of AI, making it easier for listeners to grasp intricate ideas. The visual and auditory elements can enhance learning, especially for those who might find traditional reading less engaging. Incorporating these multimedia resources into one's routine can help maintain a well-rounded understanding of AI developments.

Finally, it is crucial to approach the wealth of information available with a critical mindset. The rapid growth of AI technology often leads to exaggerated claims and misinformation. By cross-referencing multiple sources and seeking out peer-reviewed articles, individuals can develop a more nuanced understanding of the subject. Engaging in discussions and seeking feedback from knowledgeable community members can also help clarify misconceptions. Staying informed requires not only consuming information but also actively participating in the discourse surrounding AI, ensuring that individuals are well-equipped to navigate the challenges and opportunities presented by this transformative technology.

Advocating for Responsible AI Use

Advocating for responsible AI use is critical as artificial intelligence continues to permeate various aspects of everyday life. With its rapid integration into sectors such as healthcare, finance, and transportation, AI has the potential to enhance efficiency and decision-making. However, this promise comes with significant risks, including ethical concerns, biases in algorithms, and the potential for misuse. As AI technologies evolve, it is essential for individuals and communities to engage in discussions about their ethical implications and advocate for frameworks that prioritize responsible usage.

One of the primary concerns surrounding AI is the potential for bias, which can emerge from the data used to train these systems. If the data reflects existing societal inequalities, the resulting AI applications can perpetuate and even exacerbate these biases. For example, biased algorithms in hiring processes can lead to discrimination against certain demographic groups. To combat this issue, advocates for responsible AI must push for transparency in how AI systems are developed and trained. This includes encouraging organizations to disclose their data sources and methodologies to ensure accountability and fairness in AI applications.

Additionally, privacy is a key issue in the conversation about responsible AI use. The collection and analysis of vast amounts of personal data by AI systems raise questions about consent and the security of this information. Individuals must be informed about how their data is being used and have a say in its collection. Advocacy for stricter regulations and guidelines surrounding data privacy is essential in empowering individuals to protect their information in an AI-driven world. This can involve supporting initiatives that promote user rights and transparency, ensuring that technological advancements do not come at the cost of personal privacy.

Moreover, education plays a crucial role in advocating for responsible AI use. As AI technologies become increasingly integrated into daily life, it is vital for the general public to understand how these systems work and their potential impacts. Educational programs that focus on AI literacy can equip individuals with the knowledge needed to critically assess AI applications. This understanding will enable people to make informed decisions, engage in meaningful discussions about AI policies, and advocate for the ethical development of these technologies.

Finally, fostering collaboration between various stakeholders is essential for promoting responsible AI use. This includes not only tech companies and policymakers but also community members and advocacy groups. By creating platforms for dialogue and collaboration, diverse perspectives can be brought together to address the multifaceted challenges posed by AI. Such partnerships can lead to the development of ethical guidelines and best practices that reflect the values and needs of society as a whole. Ultimately, advocating for responsible AI use is a collective effort that requires active participation from all sectors of society to ensure that AI serves the greater good.

Exploring Career Opportunities in AI

As artificial intelligence continues to evolve and permeate various aspects of our lives, the career opportunities in this field are expanding rapidly. Individuals from diverse backgrounds and skill sets can find a place in the AI landscape. The demand for AI professionals is not limited to those with technical expertise; roles in project management, ethics, and user experience are also vital. This broadening of career paths creates an inclusive environment where individuals can leverage their unique strengths to contribute to AI development and deployment.

One of the most significant emerging trends in AI is the rise of interdisciplinary collaboration. Professionals in fields such as healthcare, education, and finance are increasingly working alongside AI specialists to enhance their industries. For example, healthcare professionals are utilizing AI to improve diagnostics and patient care, while educators are integrating AI-driven tools to personalize learning experiences. This trend underscores that a background in a non-technical field can still lead to meaningful contributions in AI, making it accessible for many.

In everyday life, AI is becoming an integral part of how we work and interact. Understanding the applications of AI in common tasks can help individuals identify career opportunities. For instance, roles in customer service are evolving to include AI-driven chatbots and virtual assistants, creating a need for professionals who can manage and improve these systems. Similarly, marketing is increasingly reliant on AI for data analysis and targeted advertising, indicating that skills in data interpretation and strategy are becoming more valuable.

Preparing for a future driven by AI involves continuous learning and adaptability. Individuals can enhance their employability by pursuing online courses, attending workshops, and engaging in community discussions about AI. Many platforms now offer resources tailored to beginners, allowing anyone to familiarize themselves with AI concepts and applications. Additionally, networking with professionals in the field can provide insights into emerging roles and expectations, helping individuals align their skills with market demands.

Ultimately, exploring career opportunities in AI is about recognizing the potential for growth and innovation across various sectors. As AI continues to shape our world, the importance of diverse perspectives and skill sets in this domain will only increase. By embracing lifelong learning and remaining open to new possibilities, individuals can position themselves for success in an AI-driven future, making meaningful contributions to the ongoing AI revolution.

Fostering Collaboration Between Humans and AI

Fostering collaboration between humans and AI is essential as we navigate an increasingly AI-driven world. This partnership can enhance productivity, creativity, and decision-making across various sectors. By understanding how AI can complement human abilities, we can leverage these technologies to improve our daily lives, workplaces, and communities. It is important to recognize that AI is not here to replace human efforts but to augment them, creating a more synergistic relationship that benefits everyone.

To foster collaboration, education and training play a vital role. As AI technologies continue to evolve, it is crucial for individuals to develop a basic understanding of AI principles and applications. This knowledge empowers people to interact effectively with AI systems, enabling them to utilize these tools to their fullest potential. Workshops, online courses, and community programs can help bridge the knowledge gap, ensuring that everyone, regardless of their background, can participate in this new era of technology.

Another key aspect of human-AI collaboration is the importance of transparency and trust. Individuals must feel confident in the AI systems they use, understanding how these technologies make decisions and the data they rely upon. By promoting transparency in AI algorithms and decision-making processes, organizations can foster trust among users. This trust is essential for encouraging adoption and usage of AI tools, which can lead to more innovative solutions and improved outcomes in various fields.

Moreover, encouraging a culture of creativity and experimentation is vital to harness the potential of AI. When humans and AI work together, they can generate new ideas and approaches that neither could achieve alone. Organizations should create environments that promote collaboration, allowing teams to explore how AI can enhance their work processes. This experimentation can lead to breakthroughs in problem-solving and innovation, driving progress in industries ranging from healthcare to education.

Ultimately, the goal of fostering collaboration between humans and AI is to create a balanced ecosystem where both can thrive. As we prepare for an AI-driven future, it is essential to focus on building partnerships that highlight the strengths of both humans and machines. By embracing this collaborative spirit, we can navigate the challenges and opportunities presented by AI, ensuring that technology serves as a tool for enhancement rather than a source of division. This balanced approach will help shape a future where AI contributes positively to society, improving the quality of life for all.

Chapter 8: Conclusion: Embracing the AI Revolution

The Importance of Adaptability

Adaptability has emerged as a crucial skill in the age of artificial intelligence, where rapid technological advancements are reshaping industries and daily life. As AI systems evolve, they bring both opportunities and challenges that require individuals and communities to adjust their strategies and mindsets. The ability to embrace change and learn new skills will determine how effectively people can navigate the complexities introduced by AI in various aspects of life, from work to personal interactions. Those who cultivate adaptability will not only survive but thrive in an AI-driven future.

In the workplace, adaptability is becoming increasingly important as AI technologies automate repetitive tasks and enhance decision-making processes. Employees who can quickly learn to work alongside AI tools will position themselves as valuable assets within their organizations. This means being open to upskilling and reskilling, as job roles evolve to incorporate AI systems. For instance, professionals in fields like healthcare, finance, and marketing must be willing to adopt new technologies that streamline their workflows and improve efficiency. By embracing adaptability, workers can turn potential disruptions into opportunities for career advancement.

In everyday life, adaptability plays a significant role as individuals encounter AI in various forms, such as virtual assistants, recommendation algorithms, and smart home devices. Understanding how these systems work and learning to interact with them effectively can enhance daily experiences. For example, by adapting to AI-driven personal assistants, people can optimize their schedules, manage tasks more efficiently, and even improve their overall quality of life. As AI technologies continue to integrate into our daily routines, those who remain adaptable will benefit from the convenience and efficiency these innovations offer.

Emerging trends in AI, such as machine learning and natural language processing, highlight the importance of staying informed and flexible. The landscape of AI is constantly changing, and keeping up with these developments is essential for making informed decisions. Individuals who actively seek knowledge about AI advancements and their implications will be better prepared to leverage these technologies in their personal and professional lives. This proactive approach to adaptability will not only enhance understanding but also foster a mindset that embraces change, which is critical in an ever-evolving technological environment.

Ultimately, the importance of adaptability in the face of AI revolution cannot be overstated. As society continues to integrate AI into various facets of life, those who can embrace change, learn new skills, and adjust their perspectives will find themselves at a distinct advantage. By fostering a culture of adaptability, individuals can ensure that they are not just passive observers of technological progress but active participants in shaping their futures. The ability to adapt will not only facilitate personal growth but also contribute to a more resilient and innovative society.

Shaping a Future with AI

Shaping a future with artificial intelligence involves understanding its growing role in various aspects of daily life and society at large. As AI technologies continue to evolve, they promise to transform how we work, communicate, and solve problems. This transformation is not just a distant possibility; it is happening now. From smart home devices that learn our preferences to advanced algorithms that improve healthcare outcomes, AI is already enhancing our quality of life and making tasks more efficient.

Emerging trends in AI showcase its potential to revolutionize multiple industries. In healthcare, for instance, machine learning algorithms analyze vast amounts of data to predict patient outcomes and personalize treatment plans. In finance, AI-driven analytics help detect fraud and assess risks more accurately. The automation of routine tasks is freeing up human workers to focus on more complex and creative endeavors. As these trends unfold, it is crucial for individuals to stay informed about how AI developments may impact their careers and daily routines.

AI is increasingly becoming a part of our everyday lives, often in ways we might not fully recognize. From virtual assistants like Siri and Alexa to recommendation systems on streaming platforms, these technologies are designed to enhance user experience. They learn from our interactions, gradually becoming more tailored to our preferences. Understanding these tools and their capabilities can empower individuals to leverage AI for greater convenience and productivity in their personal and professional lives.

Preparing for an AI-driven future requires proactive engagement with the technology. It is essential for people to develop a basic understanding of AI concepts and their implications. This can include taking online courses, attending workshops, or simply engaging with AI-powered tools. Additionally, fostering adaptability and a willingness to learn new skills will be crucial as job roles evolve. Embracing lifelong learning will enable individuals to remain relevant in the workforce and harness the benefits of AI innovations.

Ultimately, shaping a future with AI is a collective journey that involves individuals, businesses, and policymakers. By actively participating in discussions about ethical considerations, data privacy, and the societal impact of AI, we can help steer the technology towards enhancing human well-being. As we navigate this new landscape, it is important to remain vigilant and informed, ensuring that AI serves as a tool for positive change rather than a source of uncertainty. The future with AI is not just about technology; it is about how we choose to integrate it into our lives and communities.

Your Role in the AI Revolution

As we stand on the brink of an AI revolution, it is essential to recognize the role that each individual plays in shaping the future of this technology. AI is not just a distant concept confined to laboratories or tech giants; it is increasingly becoming part of our daily lives. From virtual assistants that help us manage our schedules to recommendation systems that suggest what to watch or buy, AI is already woven into the fabric of our everyday experiences. Understanding how AI works and its implications allows you to navigate this landscape with confidence and agency.

Emerging trends in AI suggest that the technology will only become more integrated into various aspects of life. Innovations such as natural language processing, machine learning, and computer vision are advancing rapidly, leading to applications in healthcare, education, transportation, and beyond. As a common person, you are an integral part of this evolution. By engaging with these technologies, whether through using AI-driven tools or participating in discussions about ethical implications, you contribute to shaping how AI develops and impacts society.

Preparing for an AI-driven future involves not only embracing new tools but also being proactive about the changes they bring. This includes understanding the potential job market shifts as automation takes over certain tasks. While some jobs may become obsolete, new opportunities will arise that require different skill sets. Lifelong learning and adaptability will be key attributes for thriving in this evolving landscape. By seeking out educational resources and training programs, you can ensure that your skills remain relevant and that you are prepared for the jobs of tomorrow.

Moreover, your role in the AI revolution extends to advocating for responsible AI use. As AI systems become more prevalent, ethical considerations surrounding privacy, bias, and accountability must be at the forefront of conversations. Engaging in community discussions, supporting regulations that promote transparency, and demanding ethical practices from companies can help ensure that AI serves the public good. Your voice matters in influencing how these technologies are designed and implemented, making it crucial to stay informed and involved.

Finally, embracing a mindset of curiosity and openness towards AI can transform your relationship with technology. Rather than viewing AI as a threat, consider it an opportunity for enhancement and innovation in your daily life. By exploring how AI can assist you in personal and professional tasks, you can harness its potential to improve your productivity and creativity. As you navigate this changing landscape, remember that your engagement and perspective are vital in driving the AI revolution forward, ensuring it remains a force for positive change in society.

www.ingramcontent.com/pod-product-compliance
Lightning Source LLC
Chambersburg PA
CBHW071053240526
45471CB00015B/1834